D0163530

AUG 1 4 92

Harrisburg Area Community College
McCormick Library
3300 Cameron Street Road
Harrisburg, PA 17110

COBBLESTONE LEADERSHIP

JULIAN J. ROTHBAUM DISTINGUISHED LECTURE SERIES

COBBLESTONE LEADERSHIP

*Majority Rule,
Minority Power*

BY

JAMES MacGREGOR BURNS

With L. Marvin Overby

UNIVERSITY OF OKLAHOMA PRESS:NORMAN AND LONDON

To the Memory of My Mother
Mildred Curry Burns
A Cobblestone Leader

Library of Congress Cataloging-in-Publication Data

Burns, James MacGregor.
  Cobblestone leadership : majority rule, minority power / James
MacGregor Burns.
    p.   cm. — (The Julian J. Rothbaum distinguished lecture se-
ries ; v. 3)
    Includes index.
    ISBN 0–8061–2314–1
    1. United States—Politics and government.   2. Representative
government and representation—United States. 3. Political parties—United States. I. Overby, L. Marvin. II. Title. III. Series.
JK21.B76   1990
320.973—dc20   90–50229

Cobblestone Leadership: Majority Rule, Minority Power is Volume 3 in the Julian J. Rothbaum Distinguished Lecture Series.

The paper in this book meets the guidelines for permanence
and durability of the Committee on Production Guidelines for
Book Longevity of the Council on Library Resources, Inc. ⊗

Copyright © 1990 by the University of Oklahoma Press,
Norman, Publishing Division of the University. All rights
reserved. Manufactured in the U.S.A. First edition.

CONTENTS

v

FOREWORD

AMONG THE MANY GOOD THINGS that have happened to me in my life, there is none in which I take more pride than the establishment of the Carl Albert Congressional Research and Studies Center at the University of Oklahoma, and none in which I take more satisfaction than the Center's presentation of the Julian J. Rothbaum Distinguished Lecture Series. The series is a perpetually endowed program of the University of Oklahoma, created in honor of Julian J. Rothbaum by his wife, Irene, and son, Joel Jankowsky.

Julian J. Rothbaum, my close friend since our childhood days in southeastern Oklahoma, has long been a leader in Oklahoma civic affairs. He has served as a Regent of the University of Oklahoma for two terms and as a State Regent for Higher Education. In 1974 he was awarded the University's highest honor, the Distinguished Service Citation, and in 1986 he was inducted into the Oklahoma Hall of Fame.

The Rothbaum Lecture Series is devoted to the themes of representative government, democracy and education, and citizen participation in public affairs, values to which Julian J. Rothbaum has been committed throughout his life. His life-long dedication to the University of Oklahoma, the state, and his country is a tribute to the ideals to which the Rothbaum Lecture Series is dedicated. The books comprising the series make an enduring contribution to an understanding of American democracy.

CARL B. ALBERT

Forty-sixth Speaker
of the
United States House of Representatives

COBBLESTONE LEADERSHIP
FOR AMERICA?

THE LECTURES I GAVE at the University of Oklahoma in 1987, as expanded in this volume, centrally concerned the question of the democratization of American government. Little did the audience or I know at that time—nor possibly could we have imagined—that the next great lesson in democratization would take place not in the United States but in the Soviet Union and Eastern Europe. Political systems that had appeared static, rigid, and impervious to change suddenly and dramatically opened up and spawned an extraordinary sequence of revolutionary alterations in their political and constitutional arrangements. Meantime, Americans did not make—perhaps they did not want to make—any fundamental alterations in their own structures of politics and government.

What unleashed these sensational changes in Europe? They typically were triggered by top leaders such as Gorbachev. But these leaders were responding to deeply felt needs and grievances among the public. And once the top leaders took limited steps toward reform, the "masses" took over. They flooded through the cobbled streets of ancient capitals, massed on the paving stones of central squares, and occasionally threw a torn-up cobblestone at a hated government building. Week after week, during late 1989, we watched on television the marchers gathering by the tens and hundreds of thousands in front of some gray edifice of governmental or party power, demanding that the moderate reformers move faster, insisting finally on basic institutional changes.

These were the cobblestone leaders. Some who only months before had been in jail, their protests stifled, their books or plays banned, their churches closed, were suddenly catapulted into power. They could be strong leaders because they had strong followers—indeed, followers acted also as leaders. I happened to be in Moscow and Leningrad when the First Congress of People's Deputies opened and cobblestone leaders from the cities, along with "grass-roots" representatives from the country, electrified the nation and the world with their speeches, many of which were critical of the leadership. I watched the enthralled Muscovites. Street crowds followed the proceedings on shop-window televisions; academics crowded into the director's office, with the one television set in the Institute; maids in hotels put down their dust mops and sat in the hotel guest lounges to watch televised coverage of the parliamentary proceedings.

No wonder the Soviet people were excited. What they were watching turned out to be a momentous step in a series of unprecedented Soviet reforms. In 1986 the Communist party granted more responsibility to local assemblies; the first experimental multi-candidate elections were held in some local districts the following year. In 1988 a special party conference approved sweeping political reforms designed to shift power from the party to the government. Later that same year, in October, constitutional amendments were proposed to convert the rubber-stamp parliament to an authentic, almost full-time, legislature. In 1989 the nation held its first multi-candidate elections for parliament, in which scores of party leaders were defeated. When the First Congress of People's Deputies convened, the nation's first parliamentary opposition party, the Inter-Regional Group, was founded to challenge the Communist leadership. Then, in early 1990, there was a series of more spectacular events: the meeting in Moscow of Reform Communists to write an alternative party platform; the marching of hundreds of thousands of "cobblestone leaders" through Moscow to demand democratic reform; the appeal by Gorbachev to Communist Party leaders to give up their exclusive hold on power; and finally, agreement by the Communist Party to adopt a draft platform that would open the way to a multi-party system.

Most of the East European countries were undergoing similar changes, in different combinations and permutations, and in diverse sequences, during this period. The extraordinary aspect of these changes was their *systemic* nature. The reformers were not "tinkering" or "window-dressing"; they proved to have an instinct for the institutional jugular. This was demonstrated most convincingly by their awareness of the need to work in parallel and coordinated fashion on both governmental and party modernization.

Watching these momentous developments from inside the Soviet Union and then from my side of the Atlantic, I could not but reflect on the glacial slowness of institutional reform in the United States as against that in the Soviet Union and Eastern Europe. In this century we have had but three "structural amendments" to the Constitution: election of senators by popular vote rather than by state legislatures (1913), revisions of presidential succession and related arrangements (1933 and 1967), and the prohibition of presidential third terms (1951). During this period there has been little strengthening or modernizing or restructuring of political parties; rather they have been declining before our eyes. Electoral reforms—amendments to permit women, those eighteen to twenty-one years old, and (in effect) blacks and ethnic minorities to vote—have taken place, but these essentially allowed broader voting cohorts to carry on political business through the old governmental and party vehicles.

Given the fast pace of democratization and modernization abroad, compared with our own glacial speed, what advice

might we offer cobblestone leaders as they go about restructuring their polities? Not too much, for we Americans and other
Westerners have been all too ready to offer prescriptions for
political reform and reorganization that might not fit into other
and different cultural contexts. But two suggestions might
have almost universal applications.

First and above all, every new democracy needs a bill of
rights—a guarantee of civil, political, social, and economic
freedoms. The Europeans may have to insist on it. In 1787,
when the Founding Fathers left a bill of rights out of their Constitution, our own cobblestone leaders demanded and got it.

The second imperative: there must be an opposition party—
and a strong one. The Communist parties in Eastern Europe,
as we see, are learning this lesson. In this country, people at
the grass roots acted under the leadership of Jefferson and
Madison to establish the opposition Republican Party in the
1790s. But the crucial moment came in 1800 when the Federalists, having lost to the Republicans, were willing to turn over
the presidency to men they feared and despised.

These lessons have been especially relevant to the Soviet
Union, since its Central Committee voted to surrender the
Communist Party's monopoly on power and to permit other
parties to compete for the first time since the Bolsheviks con-
solidated their power in 1917–18.

That Soviet intellectual leaders, at least, grasp the importance of grass-roots or cobblestone leadership is apparent
from comments made early in 1990 by two Soviet students
knowledgeable about both American and Soviet politics.
Georgiy Arbatov and Eduard Batalov, head and section head
respectively of the Soviet Institute of U.S.A. and Canada
Studies, wrote:

> The logical continuation of the course toward the emancipa-
> tion of mass social organizations lies in an extensive develop-
> ment of the political and social activity of the mass of the
> people. Our spring of restructuring was marked by the ap-
> pearance—for the first time in many years—of tens of hun-

dreds of spontaneous political clubs, associations, people's fronts, and other voluntary groups. They provided an outlet for the political energy of the masses that has accumulated over the long years of Stalinism and stagnation, an outlet for people's desires to express themselves and to listen to others, and to help the party and state make a reality out of what has been begun. These organizations do not have political experience and, as yet, there is nowhere for them to acquire it; they may make mistakes and get lost; and sometimes they will come into conflict with state organs. But, it is important today that we neither overestimate nor ignore their mistakes and shortcomings, that we do not swaddle them with prohibitions and do not intimidate them—in short, that we do not ruin and trample down these shoots of people's self-government, and do not sow disbelief in the minds and hearts of the young people who constitute the popular base of these organizations.

Do we have anything else to offer Eastern Europe as a political model? Very little. Oddly, we face the need to make the same kinds of changes—constitutional, party, electoral—that Eastern European leaders do.

Constitutional: Our system of checks and balances, with the resulting fragmentation of power, frustrates leadership, saps efficiency, and erodes responsibility.

No wonder that virtually all nations making a choice of constitutions since World War II have selected the parliamentary system over our eighteenth-century-style separation of presidential, congressional, and judicial power. The Soviets early in 1990 adopted a strong presidential system, but one seated in essentially parliamentary institutions.

Party: Both the Democratic and Republican parties have steadily wasted away at the grass roots. As organizations, they have lost the key functions of recruiting leaders, standing behind them in office, and taking responsibility for their performance.

The parties have largely given up their historic job of bringing out the vote, as indicated by the steady drop in turnouts in recent decades. In effect, the governing party is not governing and the opposition party is not opposing.

As I write, the Democrats cannot even get together in opposition to a Bush administration proposal to reduce the capital-gains tax that Franklin D. Roosevelt, Harry S Truman, and other Democratic Party heroes would have effectively denounced as a "soak-the-poor" bill.

Electoral: Memories of the 1988 election are so vivid that few need to be reminded of the problems—domination by the media and money; the "long ballot" that bewilders voters; the avoidance of real issues; and the endless demagoguery, sensationalism, and trivialization. One archaic feature of the constitutional system, the Electoral College, should be put into the Smithsonian Institution before it distorts the presidential vote once too often.

Will we stick with our nonegalitarian, horse-and-buggy political system while Eastern Europeans democratize and modernize theirs? Probably. Most of our officeholders are not likely to alter arrangements that help sustain them in power.

The main hope would lie in the American equivalent of cobblestone leadership. Locked away—in union locals, peace groups, church congregations, local party committees, student societies, community action and neighborhood improvement associations, environmental action groups—is a vast potential for political leadership and change.

I spell out my own agenda for reform in later pages. As a thumbnail summary here: I favor strengthening our parties at every level; cutting down election costs and corruption; attracting to the polls the missing 50 percent of the potential electorate; creating four-year congressional terms that coincide with presidential terms; and abolishing archaic minority devices (such as the two-thirds Senate vote needed to ratify treaties), substituting simple majorities in both houses.

The Soviets, Czechs, Poles, East Germans, and Romanians have been striving for liberty and equality by reshaping their political institutions. We can, paradoxically, learn from them,

but only within the framework of American values of majority rule and minority power, both enhanced by our own kind
of cobblestone leadership.

Putting lectures into book form always poses a dilemma for
the speaker and would-be author. A lecture should not run
more than the proverbial forty-five or fifty minutes, but it is
impossible to pack as much information and as many ideas
into a relatively brief lecture as one would wish. I have tried
to solve this dilemma by asking Professor L. Marvin Overby
to spell out some of the key ideas and information in the lectures at greater length. I want to thank Professor Overby for
his major substantive as well as research and editorial contributions to this work, which represents a collaboration between the two of us. Both he and I would like to thank Jackie
Johnson for her valuable research assistance. I also wish to
thank Dr. Ronald M. Peters, Jr.; Kimberly Wiar; George W.
Bauer; Mildred Logan; Julian J. Rothbaum; and the Honorable
Carl Albert, former speaker of the United States House of
Representatives, for their contributions to this work and for
their unfailing hospitality.

The quotation from Georgiy Arbatov and Eduard Batalov is
from "The Evolution of the Soviet State," in *Kettering Review*,
Winter 1990, page 18. I used some paragraphs from this introduction in an article I wrote for *The New York Times*, February 8, 1990, titled "U.S., Model for Eastern Europe?"

COBBLESTONE LEADERSHIP

CHAPTER 1

THE CONSTITUTIONAL BACKGROUND: CELEBRATION AND CEREBRATION

SINCE 1987 MARKS THE BICENTENNIAL of the United States Constitution, it is only appropriate that the theme of this year's lectureship concerns our Constitution. In these lectures I will address some of the major constitutional issues I see as having currency in this year of reflection on our governmental tradition.

For the past several years I have served as a cochairman of America's Project '87, which has been involved in organizing and coordinating a number of events to mark this two hundredth anniversary of our constitutional order. Before turning to what is, in effect, one of the last events in this commemorative year, I would like to share with you some of my ruminations about the quality of our observance of the occasion.

The past fifteen or so years have been challenging for all of us, but in the midst of momentous and often tumultuous events, we, as a nation, have taken time to celebrate our founding. We all enjoyed the tall ships and fireworks that marked the bicentennial of the Declaration of Independence, and the gala events surrounding the one hundredth birthday of the Statue of Liberty. Then we looked forward to this year, the bicentennial of our true birth as a nation in 1787. When I was at the University of Oklahoma several years ago meeting with a group of interested students, I expressed the hope that the 1987 commemoration would be marked not only by celebration, but also by *cerebration*. I have urged people around the country to honor the founding fathers by imitating them: by standing back from the exigencies of the here and now, by stepping away for a moment from the existing political reality and looking at it not only benevolently, but also critically. I have challenged people to show their capacity to extricate themselves intellectually and imaginatively from our system and to make judgments about it. I believe that this is where the commemoration of 1987 has failed.

Apart from a few lonely voices crying in a modern wilderness, asking that certain aspects of our Constitution and our constitutional order be reexamined, there has been little of the critical discourse I had hoped for. In fact, we have seen the renewal of what I believe is a very understandable phenomenon—Constitution worship. I say it is understandable because there is much about the document and the men who created it that is indeed admirable. Those of us who have undertaken academic research in this area, who have gone back through the correspondence of the founders and have spent our time in the archival records of the period, are ourselves susceptible to this malady. Certainly no one has exaggerated the genius of the founders. They really were as talented, as wise, as forward-looking as they are reputed to have been. One can see this from their correspondence; these busy men—business leaders, lawyers, scholars, planters—spent untold hours penning out their ideas over a period of years in what became a grand, collective effort to improve the quality of their regime. This effort, of course, culminated in the summer of 1787 when together they created the document whose birthday we have commemorated this year.

As we enter our third century of constitutional government, however, we must remember that the world of the founders is not our world. The institutions and processes they created may not be fully appropriate to the new age, at least not without some alteration. I will argue over the course of this discussion that some such alterations have occurred over time during our two-hundred-year history, but that we cannot afford to be complacent. The challenges that face us in the years ahead will demand that we understand better not only what is right with our style of government, but also what its limitations are and what may yet require further revision or amendment. With this in mind, let us look at our Constitution, not merely as the document produced by the founders in 1787, but also as it has been altered over time, beginning with the addition of an official Bill of Rights in 1791. This not only will allow us a better, more critical appreciation of the Constitution, but will also begin to provide some illumination of the role individual rights play in a republican system. I plan to show how our system—beginning with the Bill of Rights—has adapted itself to increasingly egalitarian historical pressures by grafting guarantees of rights onto the main trunk of the Constitution.

We are probably well advised at the start to do a little review of history and recall some basic facts concerning the Constitution. First, we must bear in mind that the framers' intention was to establish a representative system of government. In itself this was not a terribly difficult intellectual task since the notion of representation was not entirely new, having been around at least since the time of Thomas Hobbes. The genius of the founders was in establishing not a system of representation, but of representations, in the plural. They planned a nexus of representative institutions—the presidency, the House of Representatives, the Senate—each with different constituencies and constitutional authority, that would share power in a carefully crafted array of checks and balances.

Second, while the founders were concerned that the people be represented by, and have a voice in, government, they were equally concerned that this popular voice not be too loud. Today many leading patriots seem to have been profoundly inegalitarian in their political outlook. Elbridge Gerry, of Massachusetts, for instance, argued that "[t]he evils

we experience flow from the excess of democracy."[1] Roger
Sherman, of Connecticut, echoed a similar theme when he
contended "the people should have as little to do as may be
about the government."[2] Finally, Alexander Hamilton argued
vehemently during the Constitutional Convention against
the "vices of democracy" and in favor of a governmental system close to that of Great Britain, including a president for life
with absolute veto power. He even went so far as to maintain
that "[t]he people are turbulent and changing; they seldom
judge or determine right."[3] Then, too, as they sat in Philadelphia in the summer of 1787, the founders were much concerned about an incident that had occurred in western Massachusetts earlier that year. The name of Daniel Shays is
familiar to all of us, especially those who have studied American history. Although it was not much of an uprising, Shays'
Rebellion sent shock waves through the new states. Leading a
band of economically distressed farmers, Shays and others
rampaged across western Massachusetts, throwing unsym-
pathetic judges from their courtrooms and attacking the arsenal at Springfield, to back up their demands for debt relief
and more economic support from the state. Although eventually suppressed by the commonwealth's militia, Shays'
Rebellion had two profound impacts upon the members of
the constitutional convention. It gave them cause to pause
over the dangers of mob rule and called into question the ability of the individual states in the Confederation to protect
themselves from internal turmoil. Both of these concerns are
clearly addressed in the system established by the Constitution.

Third, there are two questions that I will not address at great
length here, but that will provide points of departure for the

[1] Quoted in James Madison, *Notes of Debates in the Federal Convention of 1787*
(New York: W. W. Norton and Co., 1987), 39.
   [2] Ibid.
   [3] Quoted in Max Farand, ed., *The Record of the Federal Convention of 1787*
(New Haven: Yale University Press, 1966), 1:299.

rest of the discussion. First, "Is ours a truly representative system?" Can a system as porous as ours, so exposed to specific,
parochial interests, be representative of the whole nation? We
need to ponder whether our modern participatory system has
facilitated or stunted the process of representation. Second,
"How representative were the framers themselves?" Many
scholars have worked on this question and some, like Charles
Beard, are best known for their answers to it. I agree with
Beard that there is clear indication that the founders were—at
least in terms of income, education, social standing, and the
like—signally unrepresentative of the American population of
the 1780s. In fact, an apt summary description of the framers
that I have often used is that they were "well bred, well fed,
well read, and well wed." Almost without exception their
backgrounds were semiaristocratic. They were an affluent lot
and marvelously well educated. Of the fifty-five delegates, the
great majority would by today's standards be multimillion-
aires, at least in land holdings. Most had been trained in the
tutorial method with its rigorous one-to-one student/teacher
ratio, which is particularly impressive for us in a day when we
settle for thirty-to-one, forty-to-one, or some other scan-
dalously high figure. And, they were well wed due to the marvelous colonial custom of gentlemen wedding ladies who
could bring to the marriage a dowry of two or three thousand
productive acres somewhere in Tennessee or Kentucky. This
often freed the husbands to devote their leisure time to the
more important work of reflective citizenship! I hope I will be
forgiven for saying this, but I think it a wonderful custom that
should be revived.

But I digress. If I have a disagreement with Beard, it would
be that I wonder—even if the founders cannot be said to be
representative in the narrow sense of, for instance, a Gallup
Poll—whether they were representative in a broader and
more important sense. Did they stand so magnificently for
the heritage of liberty, tolerance, and the fundamental equality of mankind that we should find them wanting for not

having been a cross section of the American public? In a sense, we honor them most for having risen above that and having represented not only the present but the future needs of Americans. Should it, in short, concern us that the founders were demographically unrepresentative of their constituents?

One last basic point—our system of government has *lasted*. It is still—albeit grown up and much changed—with us. In fact, you can find evidence of this on the front page of almost every newspaper in the country on any day of the week. Stories about struggles between the Senate and the House, between the president and the Congress, are ubiquitous and provide proof that the system our founders planned with paper and pen two hundred years ago still survives in the flesh-and-blood world of the twentieth century. This point is important because it indicates that many of the deterministic doomsayers are incorrect. A leitmotif of much modern thought has been that man is a very puny creature indeed: buffeted by fate, at the mercy of his psyche, controlled by historical forces far beyond his control, very limited in his ability to affect himself or his future. To a greater or lesser extent, this has been the message of Marx, Nietzsche, Freud, and others too numerous to mention. It is encouraging and rejuvenating to think back to that time two centuries ago when fifty men demonstrated the capacity of the human mind to plan ahead, showing that men of character and intelligence can, in fact, grapple successfully with fate. I consider what they did, whatever its strengths or weaknesses today, the most brilliant example of creative political planning in the history of the western world.

With this brief review, we should move along to our primary topic. Appropriate to this venue, I think I should call the Constitution as it was written a "surrey with the fringe on top," although perhaps it should be thought of more accurately as an old farm vehicle. The Constitution's inherent system of checks and balances, of countervailing and competing powers, is reminiscent of an old farm wagon—not a wagon with a nicely matched pair of Clydesdales pulling in tandem, but a rather rickety rig with, perhaps, three poorly matched horses each pulling in a somewhat different direction. To extend the metaphor, picture also the drivers—not one, but several—each of whom has his or her hand upon a brake. It is, it seems, a rather strange contraption; one that is durable, yet rough in its ride, tending to veer back and forth, and, I contend, in need of critical reevaluation during its two hundredth birthday.

We should also note what the framers did *not* do. They did not include in the original document a bill of rights explicitly delineating the perquisites, prerogatives, and privileges of citizenship. Today, we find this omission rather odd, and this has been reflected in the nature of the commemorative events of this bicentennial year. It is striking that many of the media programs on the Constitution have not dealt very much with the new structure of government at all, but have moved along quickly to the first ten amendments—to the Bill of Rights. Now I will grant that the original document as drafted in Philadelphia makes a terribly dull read. I feel obliged to admit that I have never read the Constitution fully through in one sitting. I have tried eight or nine times, but I never get more than about half way through because after its inspiring preamble, the remainder of the document is little more than a dry listing of processes, institutions, terms of office, restrictions, and such. It is not very moving or eloquent, nor was it intended to be. Rather, it is a lawyers' document, an outline for government, a blueprint for the granting, limiting, and withholding of power. It was intended to be dull and precise, and it is. The American people know this. So, the enthusiasm they express toward the Constitution is, in large part, directed toward the Bill of Rights.

I was particularly struck by this phenomenon when I served earlier this year as an adviser to a television network that produced a three-hour documentary on the Constitution that aired in mid-September, the night before the big celebration in Philadelphia. Repeatedly I told the directors and producers that much of the material they wanted to put in about freedom of speech, freedom of religion, etc., was not even mentioned in the original Constitution. "Why don't you wait," I counseled. "Just do the Constitution of 1787 now and then you can do an entirely new media program in 1991 during the anniversary of the Bill of Rights." They did not, I fear, understand what I was talking about. The producer was extremely proud, for example, that his show was going to mention every single amendment. I told him that some of these amendments were not really all that important and that, if he were going to do that, he should at least mention all the important provisions in the body of the Constitution. He, of course, did not like that idea at all because there was something about the amendments that attracted him in a way that the original articles did not. That "something" was a set of articulated freedoms that, then and now, excite and motivate the American mind. While I am a bit amused by this proclivity to commemorate the Bill of Rights this year, before its due time, I am also enormously impressed by it. The instinct of the American people—and this is precisely what the network was responding to—to move quickly from their commemoration of the Constitution of 1787 and on to the Bill of Rights indicates the depth of their feeling for those amendments and the liberties they set forth. It indicates that the American people, at an instinctual level, understand the importance of the Bill of Rights in tempering the constitutional order and rendering it more protective of individual rights.

The American people's instinctive grasp of this point is important. An enduring theme in democratic political analysis has concerned the supposedly radical incompatibility of majority rule with individual rights. On the surface, this tension appears very real. How, for instance, can a majority truly exercise its will if many of its potential options or actions are subject to minority veto because of individual claims to inviolable rights? Conversely, how can individual rights be considered rights at all, in any meaningful sense of the term, if they are subject to the mercurial whims of shifting political majorities?

On an abstract level, this tension seems fundamental and insoluble; concomitant expansions of individual liberties and majoritarian democracy seem logically precluded. Fortunately, we do not inhabit an abstract world. All of our governmental institutions and processes, all of our ideologies and theories, play themselves out against the backdrop of a civic culture. As writers from Alexis de Tocqueville to Louis Hartz have recognized, the American political culture is a singularly tolerant and moderate one. As a result, the political majority in America—unlike those found in many other, more radical polities—has historically proven itself to be cautious, generous, and, on balance, sensitive to individual rights. To quote from Hartz, ours has been "one of the tamest, mildest, and most unimaginative majorities in modern political history."[4]

The upshot is that the American civic culture and the majorities it has engendered have alleviated, if not eliminated, the tension between rights and rule. In the American context, at least, majority rule and minority rights are not—within the normal spectrum of political activity—mutually exclusive concepts. We have witnessed the rare—if not unique—phenomenon in America of the expansion of individual rights through the extensions of opportunities for political participation. The Bill of Rights, emerging as it did from a popular groundswell of dissatisfaction over the new Constitution, started this expansion. Six subsequent events—the rise of an opposition party, the development of judicial review, the emancipation of the slaves, the enfranchisement of women, the promulgation of an economic bill of rights, and the expansion of social

[4]Louis Hartz, *The Liberal Tradition in America* (New York: Harcourt, Brace and Co., 1955), 129.

opportunities in the 1960s—have continued it. All these can be seen as further expansions of both rights and democratic participation. Although we often speak loosely of a tension between the two notions, I am convinced that in the American context the expansion of the majoritarian principle has not served to endanger minority or individual rights, but rather to strengthen them.

More on this later; first let us recall the situation the framers faced. Of the several forces at work in the 1780s pushing America toward a more unified governmental system, one of the most potent was the economic friction that existed between the states. After a number of regulatory problems emerged between Virginia and Maryland over control of the Potomac River and Chesapeake Bay, delegates from the two states met in Alexandria, in 1785, to discuss the issue. Although the two states were able to settle the matters then in question, it was obvious the underlying problems were systemic ones that required the attention of the entire nation. This awareness of systemic problems was the mark of the framers' genius. As the Alexandria meeting broke up, the Virginia legislature called for a meeting of delegates from all thirteen states to address the numerous interstate economic difficulties raised by the Articles of Confederation. This meeting eventually convened in Annapolis in September 1786, but was attended by representatives from only five states. Nevertheless, those present adopted a report authored by Alexander Hamilton that illuminated the numerous shortcomings of the Articles and began a harsh critique of the current government. What is more, the Annapolis Convention closed by issuing another call to the states to send representatives to a new convention to be charged with amending the Articles. This invitation was forwarded not only to the individual state legislatures, but also to the Confederation Congress, which on February 21, 1787, endorsed the proposal, stipulating that the new convention's portfolio was to contain authority "for the sole and express purpose of revising the Articles," not for rejecting or replacing them.[5]

Of course, the Constitutional Convention that convened in Philadelphia in May 1787, did not take this limitation seriously and promptly began not to amend the Articles, but to toss them out and begin work on a new design for government. After the Constitution was drafted by the convention, it was forwarded to the Congress, which was then sitting in New York. Unsure of precisely what to do with this document, which clearly overstepped the convention's mandate, the Congress acted very cautiously and simply sent it out to the states for their consideration and possible ratification. Since history usually sides with the winner and the Federalists eventually prevailed in their quest for ratification, we hear little today about the stiff opposition the Constitution faced as it was sent to the states. At the time, however, supporters of the Constitution were well aware of how tenuous their claims to legitimacy were, how much suspicion there was among the body politic concerning this radical proposal, and how many people were opposed to the very notion of creating a more powerful central government that could saddle them with additional taxes, responsibilities, and regulations. Large factions in the states objected to several aspects of the Constitution, and we hear echoes of these objections still resounding in the republic today.

As the states began to consider ratifying the document, this generalized and diffuse sentiment against the Constitution came to focus increasingly on the document's lack of a bill of citizens' rights. Now the framers had some good reasons for not including such a bill in the Constitution. Among other things, they argued that like many state constitutions of the time the new national constitution already contained in its

[5]See James Madison, *Debates in the Federal Convention of 1787,* ed. Gaillard Hunt and James Brown Scott (Westport, Conn.: Greenwood Press, 1920), 1v.

text a number of enumerated citizen rights. They pointed, for instance, to the guarantee of habeas corpus, the proscription against bills of attainder and ex post facto laws, and the assurance of jury trials in criminal cases. The Federalists' main argument, however, was that they were creating a government of enumerated powers only. They did not need, they maintained, a bill of rights to prevent the new federal government from doing things it was not empowered to do in the first place. True, they were asking the people to delegate power to the new government, but they were not asking for a delegation of power to do away with personal freedoms.

This point was perhaps most forcefully stated by Alexander Hamilton in *Federalist* 84. He maintained that:

> [Bills of rights] have no application to constitutions, professedly founded upon the power of the people, and executed by their immediate representatives and servants. Here, in strictness, the people surrender nothing; and as they retain every thing they have no need of particular reservations. 'WE, THE PEOPLE of the United States, to secure the blessings of liberty to ourselves and our posterity, do ORDAIN and ESTABLISH this Constitution for the United States of America.' Here is a better recognition of popular rights, than volumes of those aphorisms which make the principal figure in several of our State bills of rights, and which would sound much better in a treatise of ethics than in a constitution of government.[6]

Hamilton, that most federal of Federalists, did not stop there, however. Pushing to make his point, he contended that a bill of rights was not only unnecessary but downright insidious:

> I go further, and affirm that bills of rights, in the sense and to the extent in which they are contended for, are not only unnecessary in the proposed Constitution, but would even be dangerous. They would contain various exceptions to powers not granted; and, on this very account, would afford a colorable pretext to claim more than were granted. For why declare

---

[6] Alexander Hamilton, John Jay, and James Madison, *The Federalist* (New York: Random House, n.d.), 558–59.

that things shall not be done which there is no power to do? Why, for instance, should it be said that the liberty of the press shall not be restrained, when no power is given by which restrictions may be imposed? I will not contend that such a provision would confer a regulating power; but it is evident that it would furnish, to men disposed to usurp, a plausible pretense for claiming that power.[7]

One can imagine how specious these arguments seemed to settlers along the backwoods of the American frontier at the time. Hateful of most governments and suspicious of all, many of these people wanted protection against governmental tyranny at *any* level. They did not want and were unlikely to settle for mere reassurances that the new government would be weak and loathe to infringe upon their freedoms. Rather, they began to demand explicitly stated, active restraints on the powers of the government. As the states geared up their political machineries to consider the proposed Constitution, those suspicious of the new government and its framers approached the ratifying conventions intent upon voicing their demands for the inclusion of a bill of rights.

The period of the state ratifying conventions is one of the most ignored and least appreciated in American history. After all the scholarship that has been focused on the Constitution itself and the convention that drafted it, we still know all too little about the politics of the state conventions that ratified the document. This is unfortunate since these were impressive gatherings that brought together some of the most important political leaders in the United States. The quality of the debates in the state ratifying conventions rivaled and occasionally surpassed those of the Philadelphia convention itself. We are well advised to take a few moments and look back on a few of them.

One important state convention was Pennsylvania's. As you might expect, this convention did vote to ratify the new constitution, coming as it did from a meeting held on the

[7] Ibid., 559.

state's own soil. But this outcome was not easily achieved. In fact, the whole affair was rather ugly. The Antifederalists in Pennsylvania were deeply opposed to the new constitution and determined to thwart its ratification. Knowing themselves to be outnumbered, they decided their best chance of scuttling the Constitution was to scuttle the Pennsylvania convention. Their tactic was to deprive the ratifying convention of a quorum by simply not showing up. Not at all amused by this tactic, the majority Federalists resorted to rather harsh measures—not for the last time in American history—and instructed their bailiffs to search high and low for the Antifederalist delegates, seize them, drag them into the chamber, and literally sit on them, at least until they could be counted as present for the purposes of declaring a quorum. We find this use of violent tactics for the purpose of absolute legality all rather amusing today, even regarding it as something of an old American political tradition. But it was ominous at the time. Even though the Pennsylvania convention voted to ratify the new constitution, the grassroots suspicion, fear, and opposition that were fanned even further by that event did not bode at all well for the critical upcoming conventions. There was a growing sense of doubt as to whether the Constitution would receive the endorsement of the requisite nine states needed for ratification, much less the unanimous sanction it would need to have any realistic chance of unifying the thirteen cantankerous new states.

A second important convention—and you'll have to forgive me for a bit of parochialism here—was held in Massachusetts. This convention took place in Boston, and I recently received a copy of the convention's proceedings as a present. I had not read them before but plunged dutifully into this old book, which had been published around 1800, intending to show my appreciation for such a sensible and discriminating gift. What I found absolutely flabbergasted me. The quality of the debates, particularly on the part of some of my fellow Berkshire men from the area around Williamstown, was astounding. In January 1788 the dozen or so delegates from Berkshire County made the arduous trip to Boston from the western part of the state, primarily to speak in opposition to ratification. Specifically, these Antifederalists, many of whom were economically strapped farmers, were quite exercised over several key provisions in the proposed constitution that they felt would affect them adversely. For instance, Article I of the Constitution gave Congress the authority to create uniform bankruptcy laws as well as to use the armed forces to suppress insurrections. Other offensive provisions were found in Article IV, which gave the new national government authority to regulate the western territories and to enforce the "full faith and credit" of each state's legal process, thus making it harder for debtors to avoid prosecution by moving from one state to another or across the western frontier.

This was not the first time inhabitants of my part of Massachusetts had taken a fairly radical stand on the political issues of their day. In fact, there is a long radical tradition in the rambunctious counties of the western part of the state. In the late 1770s and early 1780s, under the leadership of the Reverend Thomas Allen, who has been described as a "religious Jacobin," the so-called Berkshire Constitutionalists were among the state's most adamant supporters of the notions of majority rule and the social contract as the only legitimate basis for government. They agitated first for their own social compact and separation from the remainder of the Massachusetts Bay province, and later in support of state constitutional conventions in 1778 and 1780. The Berkshire delegates were no strangers to the notion of constitutional government per se—indeed, they were among its most vociferous advocates. Their opposition to the proposed national constitution of 1787 was centered on the document's many non-populist features and, specifically, its lack of a bill of rights.

The delegates from the western part of the state made their case eloquently and forcefully, and it looked for a time as if they might prevail and lead the convention to vote down the proposed ratification. This would have been a momentous development indeed, because Massachusetts was such a pivotal state. With other important conventions mere months away, an Antifederalist victory in Massachusetts might have helped shift the momentum and jeopardized the new Constitution.

As has so often been the case in American history, however, the day was saved by a propitious compromise. The Federalists and some of the Antifederalists struck a deal. This deal entailed some of the more moderate Antifederalists agreeing to support ratification of the Constitution *as written*, in exchange for a promise by Federalist leaders to work for the addition of a bill of rights after the new constitutional order was in place. This compromise was important for two reasons. First and most obviously, it facilitated the ratification of the Constitution and helped give birth to the new federal union. Second—and this is but poorly appreciated—it obviated the need for a second constitutional convention, for which some people at the time were agitating. A second convention, charged with drawing up an enumerated list of citizens' rights, would not only have been anticlimactic to the first, but also potentially dangerous. There is no reason to suppose that a second convention would have felt itself any more bound by its charge than had the first. Delegates eager to "improve" upon the structure of the original constitution might well have been tempted to tinker with it, upsetting some of the delicate compromises that have been responsible for its lasting success. So the Federalists' decision to agree to a compromise and add a bill of rights through the amendment process as soon as the new government was established represents one of the great creative acts of statesmanship in the history of the United States. That it was prompted by popular pressure—and not the independent action of the so-called political elites or the agitation of a disaffected minority—makes it all the more noteworthy.

In Massachusetts, the Constitution—along with a request

for the subsequent addition of a bill of rights—was ratified by a very narrow margin, thanks in part to the Berkshire delegates who changed their votes to support ratification. On June 21, 1788, when New Hampshire voted for ratification, the requisite nine states were on board, but the two largest states—Virginia and New York—were still debating the issue. If they failed to ratify the Constitution, regardless of what the other states did, the new union would have little chance for survival.

In Virginia, ratification was opposed by some of the state's leading patriots, including Richard Henry Lee (who had signed the Declaration of Independence and would later serve as senator), Patrick Henry, and George Mason—whom history has (improperly, perhaps) remembered as the father of the Bill of Rights. James Madison, who authored twenty-nine of the famous *Federalist Papers*, skillfully led the Federalist forces. After an opening motion by Henry to adjourn on the grounds that the Constitutional Convention had overstepped its authority was defeated, the delegates began a careful, clause-by-clause consideration of the proposed constitution.

Although proposed by the Antifederalists, this clause-by-clause approach redounded to the benefit of Madison whose clear and penetrating analysis was aided by such a structured agenda. Patrick Henry's flamboyant, but shallow, oratory, on the other hand, which preyed on general issues, themes, and fears, was inhibited by the strict rule. After Governor Edmund Randolph, who surprised many by supporting ratification, rejected a clandestine offer by Governor De Witt Clinton, of New York, to help him engineer a two-state deal demanding a second constitutional convention, the battle was all but won by the Federalists. The final blow to the Antifederalists came when Madison, who was increasingly impressed by the popular outcry for a bill of rights, committed himself to working in the new Congress for an enumeration of popular rights if Virginia would ratify the Constitution without reservations. With Madison's pledge, the convention, by an eighty to eighty-eight vote, defeated a motion to submit to the other states a list of forty proposed amendments to the Constitution prior to ratifying it. Instead, the delegates agreed to recommend the proposed amendments—many of which were based on those found in Virginia's state constitution—to the Congress for subsequent consideration. Then, almost anticlimactically, Virginia voted for ratification by an eighty-nine to seventy-nine tally.

In the other key state, New York, the Federalists were led by Alexander Hamilton and John Jay, while Governor Clinton and Melancton Smith headed the antiratification forces. As in Virginia, much of the battle turned on the question of a proposed bill of rights. The Federalists were willing to temper ratification with the recommendation that certain "useful or expedient" amendments be added later, but the Antifederalists wanted far more. Smith, for instance, proposed language that would have made New York's ratification conditional, pending the adoption of a bill of rights to be proposed by a subsequent national convention. After much hard lobbying by Hamilton, compromise wording was finally hammered out that called for ratification of the Constitution "in Confidence that" a bill of rights would be added later. With that caveat, on July 26 the New York convention voted for ratification by a narrow margin (thirty to twenty-seven), and also unanimously approved a letter to be sent to all the other states calling for a second convention to consider the proposed amendments discussed in the various state conventions.

In the final analysis, all thirteen states opted for ratification, although five did so with explicit reservations and two—North Carolina and Rhode Island—only after a bill of rights had actually been submitted to the states.

When the first Congress convened in New York in the spring of 1789, Madison made good on his promise to the Virginia ratifying convention. Trying to head off a proposal by his fellow Virginian Theodorick Bland calling for a second convention to consider a bill of rights, Madison, on May 4, 1789, announced his intentions in the Congress to press for a set of constitutional amendments. "If we can make the Constitution better in the opinion of those who are opposed to it, without weakening its frame or abridging its usefulness in the judgment of those who are attached to it," Madison said, "we act the part of wise and liberal men to make such alterations as shall produce that effect."[8] Beyond a sense of honor, however, Madison also realized the political opportunity he had been given. By championing a bill of rights, he could prove that the Constitution was a friend of liberty and concomitantly undercut the popular appeal of the Antifederalists. He suspected, correctly it turned out, that most Antifederalists were not so much proponents of individual rights as they were jealous of their own states' powers—that is, of *states'* rights. Their insistence on a bill of rights was largely a ruse. By vigorously pursuing a bill of rights, Madison could call their bluff.

Madison faced, however, an uphill fight in the Congress. Many Federalists thought that there were more important issues demanding the new legislature's attention; many Antifederalists realized that if Madison succeeded, their hopes for a second convention to undo the errors of the first were lost. The diminutive Virginian was, however, resolute in his determination to fulfill his promise and with great dexterity steered twelve proposed amendments through the House of Representatives and helped their passage through the Senate. Some of these were taken from Mason's celebrated Virginia Declaration of Rights of 1776, some from the various state ratifying conventions. Madison was able to convince the Congress not to consider "political" amendments, which were designed to alter the Constitution's basic balance of power, that many Anti-

---

[8] Quoted in Ralph Ketcham, *James Madison: A Biography* (New York: Macmillan Co., 1971), 290.

federalists supported. Finally, after much debate and many revisions, both chambers voted in late September 1789 to send a
list of twelve amendments to the states for consideration.

The debates in the state legislatures to ratify the Bill of
Rights turned out to be quite raucous. Two of the proposed
amendments—those dealing with the proportion of representatives to state population and the compensation of congressmen—were voted down by the states. In many of the
debates there was the unusual spectacle of Antifederalists,
who had so adamantly demanded a bill of rights two years
before, now desperately agitating against the amendments,
realizing that Madison had outmaneuvered them. In Virginia,
Antifederalist George Mason called them "Milk and Water
Propositions,"[9] and the state's two senators, Richard Lee and
William Grayson, forwarded the proposals to the state only
with reluctance. Nevertheless, the Antifederalists could fight
only a rearguard, delaying action against Madison's successful efforts and the growing public opinion in favor of the Bill
of Rights. With encouragement from Thomas Jefferson, the
Virginia state senate, on December 15, 1791, voted in favor
of the first ten amendments, successfully completing the
ratification process.

The upshot of this discussion is that regardless of the motives behind its support and adoption, regardless of the in-
trigues that almost scuttled it and eventually worked in favor
of its ratification, the Bill of Rights is a tremendously important addition to the Constitution. This obvious point is not
made solely on the shallow observations that it guarantees, as
it does, a set of very important rights to the American people
or that it contributed significantly to the Constitution's ratification or that it pacified restless elements of the population,
all of which it did. What is far more important, the history of
the Bill of Rights manifestly demonstrates the power of the

[9] Quoted in Robert A. Rutland, *The Ordeal of the Constitution* (Norman: University of Oklahoma Press, 1966), 297.

democratic will in the United States and the flexibility of our system to take account of that, balancing constitutional order with popular liberties within the framework of a liberal culture. In a very real and significant sense, the Bill of Rights represents a fundamental alteration in our original constitutional system that resulted from the popular realization that, in the American context, majority rule and explicit individual rights were not inherently in tension.

CHAPTER 2

MAJORITY RULE AND MINORITY RIGHTS: OUR MULTIPLE "BILLS OF RIGHTS"

THE FRAMING OF THE BILL OF RIGHTS did not come to an abrupt end in 1791 with its ratification by the states. Like the Constitution itself, it was at first merely words scratched on a sheet of parchment, symbolically important, perhaps, but little more. For the personal rights mentioned in the Bill of Rights really to mean very much, they would have to be made concrete, not abstract. The words would have to be made real, the rights exercised, tolerated, and eventually expanded. Certain prerequisite social conditions, moreover, would have to be established in order to make individual utilization of the rights even possible.

I contend that these things, in fact, were largely accomplished during six subsequent and significant episodes in American history. As a result, we have—in an analytical sense, at least—not one Bill of Rights, but seven "bills of rights." My use of the term "bill of rights" is, perhaps, rather loose. The point is not a legalistic one concerning either the constitutional status or enforceability of these subsequent "bills of rights," but rather refers to the great moments in American history when the liberties and freedoms of the American people were substantially expanded in ways that have served to fulfill the promise made by the first, formal Bill of Rights. They are important for our purposes here because they help illuminate the increasing democratization of America and—as I shall argue later—call into question the adequacy of our existing political institutions.

The second bill of rights was the rise of an opposition party within—and the toleration of this party by—the Federalist Party in the 1790s. As you will recall, George Washington was extremely suspicious of political parties—or factions, as they were then often called—and counseled both his political allies and the country as a whole against their formation. In his efforts to forestall partisan rivalry, he went so far as to place such ideological and political opponents as Alexander Hamilton and Thomas Jefferson in his first cabinet, creating in effect what we today might call a government of "national reconciliation." For a time this strategy seemed to work. The successes of the first Washington administration were impressive and served, temporarily at least, to keep nascent factional differences below the political surface. Indeed, the administration's successful assumption of the nation's debt, its salvation of the nation's credit, its ability to negotiate the entry of new states (Vermont, in 1791, and Kentucky, in 1792) into the Union, and its skillful diplomacy in regard to both Indian leaders and European nations had convinced most citizens by 1792 of the wisdom of the new federal arrangement.

There was considerably less unanimity on the subject of the Federalists' methods. The old split between the pro- and anti-Constitution forces began to reemerge over the issues of national centralization and the federal government's economic policies, many of which favored the commercial classes. One of the first outward manifestations of the increasing rift occurred in the election of 1792. While Washington was unanimously reelected president, the vice-presidential slot—then held by John Adams—was contested by George Clinton. An old Antifederalist, Clinton represented the dissatisfaction of a growing segment of the population who were coming to refer to themselves as Republicans. With Jefferson's help, Clinton offered a strong challenge to Adams, although he eventually lost the electoral college vote fifty to seventy-seven.

During the second Washington administration and the four-year tenure of John Adams, relations between the Federalists and the Republicans became more strained. Although Jefferson resigned as secretary of state in 1793, ostensibly to enjoy a more bucolic and reflective life at his beloved Monticello, political events of the day—both domestically and internationally—conspired against his expressed hopes to fade from public life. The French Revolution, for instance, with which many Republicans had sympathized, had turned increasingly violent in the early 1790s. The storming of the Tuileries Palace, the overthrow of the elected commune of Paris by an insurrectionary one, the rise to power of Danton, Marat, and Robespierre, and the execution of the royal family had profound influences both in Europe and the new United States. Federalists looked upon the atheistic orgy of prolonged mob violence with horror and feared the Republicans in their midst could lead America to the same fate. More importantly, perhaps, the revolutionary government in France got itself involved in a series of wars that further strained its relations with the United States, to which it was tied officially by treaty. Although the Washington and Adams administrations tried to maintain a posture of strict neutrality in these conflicts—especially that between France and Britain—they found themselves tested by both sides. Arguing that the cargo on neutral ships should also be considered neutral, American merchants tried to benefit from the war and expanded trade with the French West Indies. After a series of incidents with the British navy, Washington sent Chief Justice John Jay to London to negotiate a commercial treaty with Great Britain. The terms he negotiated and that were ratified by the Senate on June 8, 1795, infuriated Jefferson and his followers, who perceived them as near total capitulation to England. In effect, Jay's Treaty opened the Mississippi River to

British trade and prohibited American ships from transporting West Indian goods (for example, cotton, molasses, and sugar) to any ports other than their own. Perhaps as much as anything else, the perceived inequity of this treaty seems to have convinced the Francophile Jefferson to accept his party's draft as its presidential candidate in the 1796 election.

Although he did not actively campaign, Jefferson lost the election to Adams by only a very close sixty-eight to seventy-one vote and, under the existing electoral arrangements, became vice-president. In that office, Jefferson served as an active critic of the Federalist administration, opposing especially the infamous Alien and Sedition Acts of 1798. Blatantly partisan, these laws represented a rearguard action by an administration that saw its majority slowly slipping away. The three Alien Acts extended the residency requirement for naturalization to fourteen years and expanded the president's authority to deport or detain aliens suspected of dangerous activity. They were designed to slow the political assimilation of newly arrived immigrants (many of whom were republican-minded Irish and most of whom felt a greater affinity to the Republican than the Federalist Party) and to intimidate radical, pro-Republican French emigres to leave the country. In addition, the Sedition Act, which was actively enforced on several occasions, made publishing any false or malicious information about the government a misdemeanor and anyone conspiring to hinder the operations of government subject to heavy fines and possible imprisonment.

The Republicans responded to the Alien and Sedition Acts with the Virginia and Kentucky resolutions. Madison drafted and the Virginia state legislature adopted the first, which asserted that the acts were in violation of the Constitution and that the states might legally "interpose" their authority to prevent their execution. The Kentucky Resolution, which was secretly drafted by Vice-President Jefferson, made a much more forceful point, arguing that Congress had overstepped the limits of the Tenth Amendment in arrogating for the federal government authority that was not explicitly granted to it in the Constitution. As passed by its state legislature, the Kentucky Resolution urged other states to follow its example in considering the acts "void and of no force."[1] While Jefferson by this time had in mind his own election as president rather than nullification as the best way to solve the problem raised by the acts, he believed he had some cause to maintain his anonymity in the matter; had his role in the affair been made public, he feared he might be prosecuted under the very acts whose provisions he protested.

Jefferson was concerned that if the Federalists were allowed to enforce the Alien and Sedition Acts with impunity, there was no telling what constitutional freedoms they might turn on next. He seemed genuinely worried about the possibility that the Federalists, sensing their own electoral vulnerability, might attempt to cancel the upcoming elections and install one of their own partisans as president-for-life. But it is precisely on this point that Jefferson miscalculated and underestimated the Federalist leadership. We must remember—as Jefferson seemed to have forgotten—that the Federalist Party at that time was firmly under the control of the moderate Adams and not the radical Hamilton. Adams, scion of that distinguished Massachusetts family that has given the Republic such outstanding public service, was not the partisan operator Hamilton was. Rather, he consistently acted in what he took to be the best interest of the country, regardless of the impact on his personal political career. He saw the rising popularity of the Republicans and realized that his party would probably be defeated by Jefferson in 1800. While he was willing to do what he could to soften that defeat, Adams was unwilling to intervene to deny the Republicans their victory. Adams was correct in his predictions. In 1800, Jefferson was elected the third president of the United States, and for

[1]See Henry Steele Commager, ed., *Documents of American History* (New York: F. S. Crofts and Co., 1945), 1:178–82.

the first time in the young nation's history, one party stepped aside as another assumed the mantle of leadership.

We have become so used to such orderly transition of power from one party to another that we tend to forget how rare such events have been on the stage of world history. Countless regimes that have had pretensions to democracy have not been able to avoid crises of succession because so many "proponents" of democracy are far more tolerant of the people's will when they win than when they lose. Fortunately, in this country, the Federalist leadership knew when it was fairly licked and when it was time to go. Adams and his administration stepped aside peacefully in 1801, trusting in the process even when it did not work to their immediate benefit.

Jefferson insisted that the "Revolution of 1800 was as real a revolution in the principles of our government as that of 1776 was in its form."[2] A crucial liberty, one that had not been tested during the twelve-year hegemony of Federalist government, was established in the election of 1800—the freedom of the opposition not only to oppose, but to prevail peacefully. Not only did this constitute evidence to the world that the American polity was far more stable than it may have appeared, it was a notice to future American political leaders that they need not contemplate coups or venture violence in order to succeed. Much to the contrary, the path to political power in the United States was shown to lead directly to and through the ballot box, ensuring for generations to come the freedom of meaningful political opposition and the regular, orderly, peaceful transfer of political power.

The third "bill of rights" is the Supreme Court's decision in *Marbury v. Madison*, the case in which the great precedent for judicial review was established. As with the transfer of power from the Federalists to the Republicans in 1800, the usual

---

[2]Quoted in Daniel Sisson, *The American Revolution of 1800* (New York: Alfred A. Knopf, 1974), 21.

brief historical accounts of the Marbury decision—as well as what preceded and followed it—are often truncated and do not reflect all the significant issues that hung in the balance and little of the political skill requisite to write the opinion.

Judicial review is the authority of the courts to rule on the legality of legislation—that is, whether particular laws comport with the Constitution. By the time the Supreme Court decided the case of *Marbury v. Madison* in 1803, the issue of judicial review was not a new one. Indeed, almost two hundred years previously the British legal system had struggled with the issue in what is known as Dr. Bonham's Case. Subsequent to a grant of authority from Parliament, the London College of Physicians had found Dr. Bonham guilty of practicing medicine without a license and levied a fine against him. In deciding the case on Dr. Bonham's appeal, the celebrated jurist Sir Edward Coke, then chief justice of the king's bench, struck the Parliament's grant of authority to the College, ruling the physicians were not entitled to judge cases in which they had a stake in the outcome. Such a situation was not only unfair, Coke reasoned, but unfair to the extent that it violated common law. Even the crown and the Parliament, Coke argued, were subject to the equitability dictates of the common law, and it was within the courts' purview to rule on such matters.

Few of the framers, it seems, objected to the notion of judicial review, per se. Most realized that practical considerations dictated some institution have the authority to police the Constitution and ensure that its provisions were upheld. The question, rather, was how extensive this authority should be. Obviously, it had to be at least enough to give the judiciary power to veto threats to its political independence; this much was implicit in the very notion of separation of powers. But how much further should the power extend? Should the federal courts have it in their portfolio to rule only on merely procedural matters, that is, on whether or not the Congress in passing laws and the president in executing them followed the constitutional process? Or should the judiciary's authority also include the prerogative of ruling on substantive matters—that is, whether or not what a law attempted to do was constitutional?

These matters cut to the very heart of constitutional theory and split the founders badly. At issue was whether, in practice, the Constitution was to be considered superior to subsequent legislation and, if it was, who, in the final analysis, was to make the relevant determinations. Mentioned only briefly in the Constitution itself, judicial review seems purposefully to have been left ambiguous by the framers, perhaps in the hope that the issue could be resolved as the new nation got down to the practical business of actual governance. As it turned out, affairs were not to be nearly that simple. Many of the Federalists advocated giving the judiciary considerable power in this area. Good social contractarians, they argued that delegated powers cannot legally be exercised except under the terms on which they are commissioned; the federal courts seemed the best judges of those commissions. Writing in *Federalist* 78 Hamilton maintained that "the nature and reason of the thing. . . . teach us that the prior act of a superior ought to be preferred to the subsequent act of an inferior and subordinate authority; and that accordingly, whenever a particular statute contravenes the Constitution, it will be the duty of the judicial tribunals to adhere to the latter and disregard the former."[3]

The Antifederalists and later the Republicans, who were also good social contractarians, had a much different view of the matter. Fearful of the concentration of power in the hands of the central government, many Antifederalists argued that when delegated power was misused at the national level, it was the responsibility of the states to intervene and void such action. Indeed, as we have seen, when the Alien and Sedition Acts were passed by a Federalist Congress and signed by

[3]Hamilton, Jay, and Madison, *The Federalist* (see chap. 1, n. 6), 507.

John Adams, it was exactly such state interposition that Jefferson and Madison proposed in the Kentucky and Virginia Resolutions. As Madison put it in the Virginia Resolution: "In case of a deliberate, palpable, and dangerous exercise of other powers not granted by the [Constitution], the states . . . have the right and are in duty bound to interpose for arresting the progress of the evil."[4]

While the ideological debate between the Republicans and the Federalists over judicial review heated up during the 1790s, a number of cases related to the issue began to work their way through the federal courts. During this decade, at least three state laws were invalidated by federal judges as unconstitutional. In 1791, for instance, the Circuit Court for Connecticut ruled that a law in that state contravened the terms of the Treaty of Paris that had ended the American Revolution and hence violated the supremacy clause of the Constitution, which made national laws and treaties the "supreme law of the land." None of these cases, however, required the federal judiciary to rule on the centerpiece of the judicial review controversy—the Federalists' claim that the courts had the right to review and nullify acts of the national legislature. Since the Federalists controlled all three branches of government, this is not surprising. With the Republicans' ascendance in the election of 1800, however, the stage was set for a possible showdown on the issue.

Immediately following the Federalists' loss at the polls in 1800, President Adams attempted to soften the blow of defeat by appointing some of his fellow partisans to key governmental posts. The Federalists hoped that by filling the governmental infrastructure with their ideological compatriots they could limit what damage the radical Republicans could do, at least until their next chance to challenge Jefferson at the polls in 1804. One of these last-minute appointments went to William Marbury, who was named a justice of the peace. Al-

[4]Commager, *Documents of American History*, 1:182.

though the appointment was duly approved, signed, and sealed, the secretary of state, John Marshall, failed to deliver it to Marbury before the expiration of Adams's term. When Jefferson and his new secretary of state, James Madison, found the undelivered commission, they decided to ignore it. When he discovered what had happened, Marbury sued in federal court for a writ of mandamus to have his appointment honored.

Now, another of Adams's last-minute appointments went to his loyal secretary of state, John Marshall, who was named chief justice of the Supreme Court. Marshall had not been Adams's first choice for the post, but when the venerable John Jay declined the offer, the president chose Marshall, probably unaware how propitious the selection would be. As the nation's fourth chief justice, Marshall would preside over and guide the Supreme Court for thirty-four years, writing some of its most important decisions and, through them, influencing the development of the young nation along distinctly Federalist lines.

When the Marbury case came to the Supreme Court in 1803 after a long delay engineered by the Republicans, Marshall immediately recognized the wonderful opportunities and the dangerous challenges it offered. First, Marshall had been hoping for some time for a test case in which he could assert the Court's right of judicial review. Due to the Court's vulnerable position and the Republicans' antipathy to the notion of judicial review, however, he realized he had to pick his case with care. If, for example, the Court voided an act of Congress and demanded the administration cease and desist from enforcing it, the decision might simply be ignored, not only frustrating but inverting the precedent Marshall hoped to establish. The issue raised in the Marbury case offered Marshall a path around this problem. Marbury asked the Court, under the authority granted it by Congress in the Judiciary Act of 1789, to invoke original jurisdiction in the matter and issue the Jefferson administration a writ of mandamus demanding the appointment be honored. Marshall did not, however, believe the Act itself to be constitutional, since it granted the Court original jurisdiction in petty personnel matters, while the Constitution limited the Court's jurisdiction to only those "cases affecting ambassadors, other public ministers and consuls, and those in which a state shall be a party." In other words, Marshall saw in Marbury a brilliant opportunity to assert judicial review by refusing to act against the incumbent administration—the precedent could be established without fear of presidential or partisan contravention.

This course of action also allowed Marshall to avoid the significant personal and professional danger presented by the case. Since he had been a principal actor in the affairs leading to the case, many prominent Republicans—for reasons of partisanship as much as equity—argued that Marshall should not be allowed to sit in judgment. Indeed, the Jefferson administration was then engaged in a serious effort to drive as many Federalist judges from office as possible and mere weeks before the announcement of the Marbury decision sent an impeachment request to the House of Representatives in the case of Judge John Pickering. A conflict of interest charge in the Marbury case would have given the Republicans all the ammunition they needed to remove Marshall from his post. By refusing to support the previous Federalist administration, Marshall knew he could make any conflict of interest charge appear ludicrous.

In the end, Marshall's shrewd political decision to wait for a case like Marbury and his brilliant judicial analysis in the decision left the Jeffersonians stumped; there was little they could do given the Court's clever self-denial. Although the immediate effect of the Marbury ruling was minimal—except of course to poor Marbury—the precedent set in the case ticked away for decades, rarely used. When it was used, as in the infamous Dred Scott case, it usually was employed to limit rather than expand personal liberties. In our century, however, that historical trend has been reversed. Since the

Great Depression, the high court has shown itself quite willing to utilize judicial review to restrain the legislature when it threatens to infringe upon constitutionally guaranteed individual rights. Often, as in many notable civil rights cases, these decisions have served effectively to extend the suffrage and expand popular participation in politics. Indeed, the Marbury case, which appears countermajoritarian on its face, has in effect been employed as a precedent in this century both to extend majoritarianism and to protect individual rights. All of this vindicates, it seems, Hamilton's analysis in *Federalist* 78 "The judiciary, from the nature of its functions, will always be the least dangerous to the political rights of the Constitution; because it will be least in a capacity to annoy or injure them. . . . [T]hough individual oppression may now and then proceed from the courts of justice, the general liberty of the people can never be endangered from that quarter."[5]

The fourth entry on this list of "bills of rights" may be a bit more obvious: the emancipation of the black slaves and their subsequent reception of legal and political rights by the so-called Civil War Amendments. Together, the freeing of the slaves and the amending of the political order to include their suffrage—too often merely a formal right that has become increasingly substantive in this century—both expanded individual rights and broadened the classes of citizens participating in the nation's governing process.

Too often we think of emancipation and the passage of the thirteenth, fourteenth, and fifteenth amendments as the natural and inevitable results of our convulsive internecine struggle, the Civil War. In fact, few conclusions in our history have been less foregone or more difficult to negotiate. When the sectional conflict between the rural agrarian South and the industrializing North exploded in 1860 with the election of Abraham Lincoln, the main issues concerned economic

---

[5] Hamilton, Jay, and Madison, *The Federalist*, 504.

and intergovernmental affairs such as tariffs and the right of states to nullify national laws, not the moral issue of slavery. Even Lincoln, the Great Emancipator, was no friend of abolitionists and considered reunification of the nation more important than the emancipation of the black slaves. Repeatedly, during the early months of the war, Lincoln asserted his loyalty to the Union above all else; he was a moderate and his plan at first was for a gradual form of emancipation, which would include compensation for former slaveholders, after the salvation of the Union. While Lincoln viewed slavery as an immoral practice, he did not believe it of sufficient weight to put the Union itself at risk.

A wily politician, Lincoln believed such a middle course the most tenable one. We tend to forget today how tenuous Lincoln's hold on power was during much of the war and how war-weary the North became during the course of the great struggle. The president attempted to keep the country as united as possible through the shedding of his Republican Party label and the formation of an amorphous Union Party. In his government he tried to balance radical abolitionists with moderates while wooing border state War Democrats—many of whom owned slaves—to remain loyal to the Union. There was much talk of a negotiated peace that would repair the Union while leaving slavery unaffected, at least in the states that already allowed it.

For most of the first two years of the conflict, Lincoln resisted pressures to issue an emancipation order, fearful such a move might damage fragile relations with border states and alienate large sections of the Democratic Party. Events, however, continued to press in upon the president, making emancipation seem increasingly attractive. First, support for the war waned markedly in 1862. Confederate victories in the South—at such places as Fredericksburg, Cold Harbor, New Market, Manassas, and Murfreesboro—rendered the war increasingly costly and Democratic agitators in the North— known as Copperheads—led more people to question whether the goal was worth its high price. Lincoln recognized that a call for emancipation would elevate the moral tone of the war and give the weary nation a truly inspiring cause for which to carry on.

Moreover, the president was concerned about a possible Confederate diplomatic breakthrough that could bring England or France into the war as a Southern ally. Lincoln knew that the British navy, if it chose to do so, could easily crush the Union blockade, provide the Confederacy with much-needed materiel, and force Washington to sue for peace on Southern terms. He also knew all too well that both countries had considerable financial investments in and sympathy for the South. Britain was a major consumer of Southern cotton, and many of her political elites favored Southern politics and policies to Northern ones. Conservative Tories, for instance, identified with the old Southern aristocracy and would have applauded the defeat of the more democratically minded Union; English liberals, likewise, favored the South because of its free-trade policies, which stood it in marked contrast with the protectionist North. On the other hand, many English reformers were quite perplexed at Lincoln's early moral ambiguity on the slavery question, claiming as he did that the war was one for union, not freedom. Viewing this situation, Lincoln surmised, correctly as it turned out, that as long as the conflict remained one of Northern interests versus Southern interests, the threat of British intervention would remain a real one. With an order of emancipation, however, he could rally his English allies, undermine the moral position of the South's British advocates, and effectively keep the British—and all other European powers—neutral.

Finally, Lincoln was increasingly pressed by radical abolitionists within his own Republican Party. Led by Senator Charles Sumner, of Massachusetts, and Representative Thaddeus Stevens, of Pennsylvania, radical Republicans in the Congress led an effort late in 1861 to create a Joint Committee on the Conduct of the War and insisted on a policy to free the slaves. As the ranks of the radicals grew, Lincoln came to real-ize that he either had to back emancipation efforts or risk alienating a large number of his fellow partisans.

Sometime in the summer of 1862, Lincoln apparently de-cided to issue an order freeing slaves. He made two other cru-cial decisions, however, at the same time. One was to free only those slaves held in Confederate states; taking a like measure in the border areas would be too risky to Union sup-port there. Second, he opted to delay announcing his deci-sion until after a major Northern victory, lest it appear to lack force or be perceived as the precipitous action of a desperate nation. The Army of the Potomac provided the needed vic-tory on September 17, the bloodiest day of the war, when General George McClellan stopped Robert E. Lee's attempted invasion of Maryland and Pennsylvania at Antietam Creek. In a preliminary edict that was issued on September 22 and be-came official several months later, Lincoln ordered that "on the 1st day of January, A.D. 1863, all persons held as slaves within any State or designated part of a State the people whereof shall then be in rebellion against the United States shall be then, thenceforward, and forever free."[6]

Beneath the rhetoric, however, there remained consider-able ambiguity on Lincoln's part. He was not outlawing slav-ery by his action, but only slavery in the Confederacy, where his authority was extremely limited; enforcement of the Proc-lamation depended upon a Union victory. The status of slaves in border states such as Maryland, Missouri, Kentucky, and elsewhere was not officially altered and remained ambiguous. What is more, Lincoln made it clear that he was undertaking the measure primarily as a strategic expedient. The Eman-cipation Proclamation was issued under his authority as commander-in-chief and was justified—since many hoped it would prompt slaves to flee to the Union armies, depriving the South of vital manpower—"as a fit and necessary war

[6] Commager, *Documents of American History*, 1:420.

measure for suppressing [the] rebellion."[7] Although Lincoln was evolving in his views and increasingly coming to see slavery as a decisively moral matter, his movement was slow and always taken with one eye out for the practical political considerations.[8]

For Lincoln, the critical moment came not in 1862, when he issued the Emancipation Proclamation, but two years later, in 1864, when he sought reelection. In the months preceding the election, the president's reelection chances did not look particularly promising. The Democrats had chosen the popular war hero General George McClellan as their champion, and his peace platform resounded well in an electorate tired of casualties and of Grant's grinding pace toward Richmond. Although Lincoln had shored up his moderate support by choosing Andrew Johnson, the slave-owning military governor of Tennessee, as his running mate, he felt by midsummer that the electoral tides were against him and that he would not win reelection. On the recommendation of Henry J. Raymond, the *New York Times* editor who served as chairman of the Republican National Committee, Lincoln drafted a letter to Jefferson Davis suggesting his willingness to consider a cessation of hostilities with reunification as the only requisite for peace. All other issues—including the continuation of slavery—would be negotiable. In a momentous move, however, Lincoln decided not to send the letter, feeling it would be morally wrong to abandon his emancipation stance, whatever the electoral consequences.

We all know, of course, that Lincoln was wise to stand on

---

[7]Ibid., 421.

[8]Barely six days after the announcement of the Emancipation Proclamation, for instance, the state legislature in Lincoln's home state of Illinois passed a resolution condemning the measure. The Proclamation, it insisted, constituted "a gigantic usurpation, at once converting the war, professedly commenced by the administration for the vindication of the authority of the constitution, into the crusade for the sudden, unconditional and violent liberation of 3,000,000 negro slaves." See Commager, *Documents of American History*, 1:422.

his principles. He won the election of 1864 by 400,000 votes, and in the spring of the following year the Northern forces finally defeated the Confederacy's badly depleted armies. The war was over, and the Southern slaves were free. For a few days, at least, the country could celebrate.

With Lincoln's death at an assassin's hand and the passing of the leadership mantle onto Andrew Johnson's shoulders, however, severe tensions within the Republican Party became more obvious. After a brief honeymoon period in which the Radicals and Johnson, the fiery opponent of the Southern aristocracy and champion of the small farmer, got along very well, the Congress and the president split over the issue of the treatment of blacks. Many Radicals felt that Johnson was more interested in punishing the Confederate leadership than in promoting or protecting the rights of the South's black population. Although the thirteenth amendment, which officially outlawed slavery throughout the United States, sailed through Congress and was ratified by the requisite number of states on December 18, 1865, Reconstruction was beginning to bog down. Beyond the freeing of the slaves, it was quite unclear—and disputed—what role the federal government should play in aiding the new "freedmen."

Radical Republicans pushed for an active federal presence in the South to guarantee newly emancipated blacks de facto as well as de jure freedom and equality. Many of them backed extensions of the suffrage, massive educational efforts, and land redistribution. In the nation as a whole and in the South in particular, however, support for these aims was faltering. Efforts to educate emancipated blacks met with stiff resistance in the South, where it was feared education would "ruin" them for manual labor. As the old Southern leadership began to reestablish itself in local and state politics, efforts were made to deny housing in white neighborhoods to whites who taught blacks and then to arrest them as vagrants when they took up residence in black homes. Neither was there much progress on the issue of providing new freedmen with their own land from confiscated plantation holdings. Although some land was given to blacks during and immediately after the war, Johnson's amnesty arrangements restored land to any Southern white who took the requisite loyalty oath. Furthermore, many of the moderate and some of the radical reconstructionists shuddered at the very thought of property redistribution and the precedent it could set in other areas. Despite the impassioned pleas of many radicals and the profound need of many former slaves, no systematic land confiscation or redistribution efforts were undertaken in any state of the old Confederacy.

The suffrage issue was more complicated. Although there was considerable sympathy in the North for enfranchising blacks in the South, many Northerners did not want suffrage extended to blacks in the North, feeling—ironically—that that would be an infringement on their states' rights. As the fourteenth amendment worked its way through the Congress in 1866, proponents had to soft-peddle its impact on states' rights and alter its language to remove its explicit guarantee of black suffrage. Although eventually passed by the Congress and ratified by the requisite number of states, the fourteenth was bitterly opposed by President Johnson, who urged states not to vote for ratification. Ulysses Grant, the Republicans' choice to replace Johnson as president in 1868, took a similar position on the issue of black suffrage: it was fine for the South, but not for the North. The Republican platform summed up the Party's position: "The guarantee by congress of equal suffrage to all loyal men at the South was demanded by every consideration of public safety, of gratitude, and of justice, and must be maintained; while the question of suffrage in all the loyal states properly belongs to the people of those States."[9]

After Grant's election in 1868 and the ratification of the

[9]Henry Harrison Smith, *All Republican National Conventions from Philadelphia* (Washington, D.C.: R. Beall, 1896), 31.

fourteenth amendment, incorporating the bill of rights on the state level, the focus of Radical Republicans turned to an all-out effort to pass a suffrage amendment. Still a potent force in Congress and many states, the Radicals were able to convince many of their copartisans that black enfranchisement was not only morally correct, but politically practical in the North, where black populations in urban centers were growing and represented a large untapped pool of votes. Even so, crafting and passing the amendment took much effort. Sponsors were forced to compromise on the scope of the law and its enforcement. The federal government was given no explicit power to secure black suffrage; instead, both the national and state governments were enjoined from denying it. What is more, the amendment is moot on the point of the denial of suffrage opportunities by private parties, and proponents were pressured into dropping clauses that would have specifically proscribed property qualifications and literacy tests. Although Radicals were euphoric when the fifteenth amendment was ratified in 1870, the last of the Civl War amendments was soon to be circumvented by exactly those types of actions that its sponsors could not find the votes to forbid.

The history of the emancipation period is, then, highly checkered. Lincoln's transformative leadership, which eventually led him to prevail by subordinating practical considerations to moral objectives, could not be maintained in the postwar years. There was a critical failure of leadership in the reconstruction period. As Kenneth Stampp has argued, the Radicals "seemed to have [had] little conception of what might be called the sociology of freedom, the ease with which mere laws can be flouted when they alone support an economically dependent class, especially a minority group against whom is directed an intense racial hatred."[10] Although great formal strides were made in this period, most of

---

[10] Kenneth Stampp, *The Era of Reconstruction, 1865–1877* (New York: Alfred A. Knopf, 1975), 129.

the national leadership failed to recognize the critical role federal authority has to play in such situations, where, given the sociological forces at work, libertarian and egalitarian goals cannot be achieved otherwise.

Still, constitutional precedents that would take on flesh and blood a century later were placed on the books, and a slow process of equalization in the South was begun. The rights that were formally granted at this time would be crucial in expanding black political participation in the next century. So again we see the pattern: not a conflict between rights and democracy, but rights in concert with—in this case, perhaps a requisite for—democracy.

The fifth entry in the list of "bills of rights" is the expansion of the franchise to women in the wake of the suffragette movement. Our earlier description of the fifteenth amendment as extending the suffrage to freed slaves is a bit of shorthand. In fact, to the disappointment of many women activists of the time, the fifteenth extended the suffrage only to freed black males; black females, like their white sisters, were not enfranchised under the amendment. Many women in the North who had worked hard for the abolitionist cause and many women on both sides of the Mason-Dixon line who had borne great suffering and made tremendous sacrifices during the Civil War were justifiably disappointed that the language of the postwar amendments was not interpreted so as to grant women the vote.

The continued exclusion of women from most forms of political participation in the postwar years was merely one of the many setbacks the women's suffrage movement faced in its nearly one-hundred-year battle for the right to vote. When the movement was started in the early years of the nineteenth century, the status of women in the United States was inferior to that of men on almost every level. No college in the country accepted female students, and most professions were likewise exclusively male. Legally, a woman's property passed to her husband at the time of marriage, and the husband had sole legal responsibility for any children in the marriage. In many instances a husband was responsible for his wife's behavior, and women, of course, had no voting rights at all.

Throughout the 1800s, women's groups organized for a variety of reform activities, usually concentrating on abolition and female suffrage. In 1848, in Seneca Falls, New York, the first women's rights convention issued a "Declaration of Sentiments" that called for suffrage and much more, outlining an ambitious ideology of and agenda for women's rights. From the beginning, however, the movement was marked by determined external opposition and serious internal cleavages. The largest external obstacle was the widespread perception that women had a proper—and extremely circumscribed—place in community life. For a majority of people, both male and female, at this time, women were seen as the pillars of home and hearth. As former president Grover Cleveland put the point in the May 1905 edition of the *Ladies Home Journal*,

> [the suffrage movement has a] dangerous, undermining effect on the characters of the wives and mothers of our land. . . . It is a thousand pities that all the wives found in such company cannot sufficiently open their minds, to see the complete fitness of the homely definition which describes a good wife as "a woman who loves her husband and her country with no desire to run either."[11]

The women's suffrage movement faced other external obstacles as well. Many labor organizations were dubious of or outright opposed to the movement because they feared the low-wage competition liberated women might offer. Many business interests were worried that the movement might lead to stricter child-labor laws. The political parties of the day were reluctant to take up the cause of women's suffrage because, among other things, it represented the type of po-

[11] Grover Cleveland, "Women's Mission and Women's Clubs," *Ladies Home Journal* (May 1905), 3.

tential realignment issue that could irrevocably alter the political landscape, perhaps to their detriment.

Internally, the suffrage movement was badly split along a number of different dimensions at different times. There was, for instance, an ongoing disagreement between "hard core" and "social" feminists within the movement; the former agitated exclusively for women's rights, the latter for social reform more generally or for women's rights as a way to address larger social wrongs. There were those who favored independent political action, such as those who formed the National Woman's Party, and those who preferred to work within the existing major parties. There were, in addition, those who believed in elite political action, such as the founders of the Women's Joint Congressional Committee, who often argued with more grass-roots, bottom-up style organizers, such as the League of Women Voters. The disunity of the suffrage movement reflects, in part, the factious nature of the American left, which, unlike its British counterpart, could often find little basis for common action or support for common issues.

After the Civil War and the failure of women to be included in the fifteenth amendment, one of the principal issues confronting the women's movement was what type of strategy to use in taking its case to the American people. One organization, the National American Woman Suffrage Association, led by the social reformers Lucy Stone and Julia Ward Howe, committed itself to state-level efforts, despairing of a constitutional amendment. Its rival was a more radical organization, the National Woman Suffrage Association, led by such militants as Elizabeth Cady Stanton and Susan B. Anthony. The NWSA, in contrast to the NAWSA, demanded more prompt and sweeping reforms than those promised through state-by-state action and agitated for a constitutional amendment granting women the vote. Both efforts enjoyed some success in the late 1800s. In 1878 the first proposed amendment to extend the suffrage to women was introduced into the Senate,

and in 1889 the full Senate considered a proposed amendment on the floor, but voted it down. On the state level,
women's groups had some success in the more egalitarian
West. By the turn of the century, four states—Wyoming,
Utah, Colorado, and Idaho—had enfranchised women. In the
early years of the new century, Washington, California, and
Illinois also moved to extend the suffrage to women.

By 1915, however, the suffrage pace had slackened, and the
women's movement faced opposition on both the national
and state levels. Nationally, although Roosevelt's Progressive Party voted in 1912 to become the first major party to
support extension of the suffrage, congressional action continued to be blocked, in part by the conservative Southern
committee chairmen who had come to power with the new
Democratic majority in the teens. In 1914 yet another proposed amendment was overwhelmingly defeated in the Senate. On the state level, progress was also slow, especially in
the Southern legislatures. Although both the Democratic and
Republican platforms in 1916 endorsed state action on suffrage, that path seemed increasingly unattractive to the leaders of the movement.

At this moment of its greatest challenge, the women's suffrage movement produced a leadership cadre equal to the
task. With the deaths of Stanton and Anthony in the first decade of the new century, a new generation of leaders came
to power in the movement, militant leaders with well-honed
political and organizational skills. Carrie Chapman Catt, a
woman of fierce determination, became head of the National
American Woman Suffrage Association, and a new, more militant organization—the Congressional Union for Woman Suffrage—was founded and headed by Alice Paul, a veteran of
the suffrage movement in Britain. Also fortunate was the
presence of Woodrow Wilson in the White House. Although
Wilson had long favored a state-by-state approach to suffrage
and had to step but gingerly on the issue due to his need for
strong support among Southern conservatives, the move-

ment's leadership felt he could be a valuable ally. Women in states that allowed them to vote had supported Wilson strongly in 1914, and many felt he owed them a debt when he stood for reelection in 1918.

In the late teens, the suffrage movement began one last drive for a constitutional amendment—the "Susan B. Amendment," as it was called. The NAWSA organized both state and local lobbying efforts. Nationally, one of the most able lobbyists was Helen Gardener, a friend of Wilson's and a neighbor of House Speaker Champ Clark. Gardener lobbied the president formally, urging him to see women's suffrage as a valuable war expedient, and the speaker more informally, usually tempting him with choice Southern delicacies prepared by her cook. In January 1918, after much effort by the movement and its political allies, the Susan B. Amendment came before the House, where it was passed by exactly the two-thirds majority necessary—274–136. The vote of Speaker Clark was ready if necessary, but was not needed. As the battle moved to the Senate, the movement redoubled its effort. Called upon to persuade undecided votes, Wilson even made an eloquent, personal appeal to the entire chamber: "We have made partners of the women in this war; shall we admit them only to a partnership of sacrifice and suffering and toil and not to a partnership of privilege and of right?"[12] Still, the Susan B. Amendment failed in the Senate by two votes.

By this time, however, the opposition had spent itself, and, given their role in the war effort, the case for women's suffrage was stronger than ever. In June 1919, both houses of Congress finally passed the proposed constitutional amendment and sent the measure to the states. Despite fierce opposition in the South, the requisite three-quarters of the states ratified the proposal rather quickly. A little more than a year after it cleared the Congress, on August 26, 1920, the

[12] *Congressional Record,* 65th Cong., 2d sess., 30 September, 1918, 10929.

nineteenth amendment became the law of the land, stating that the "right of citizens of the United States to vote shall not be denied or abridged by the United States or by any State on account of sex."

It had taken almost one hundred years of organized effort, great personal sacrifice, and the surmounting of hundreds of frustrations and setbacks to enfranchise women voters. Although the suffrage movement's leaders had played the game of expedient politics, trading votes and making deals to prevail in our veto-ridden system, the nature of the pluralist system also undermined their efforts to forge effective, ongoing coalitions with other groups such as organized labor, recent immigrants, newly enfranchised blacks, or any existing political party. As a result, although the nineteenth amendment undoubtedly expanded liberty and enlarged democracy, the suffrage movement's long-term ability to have an impact on the social and humanitarian issues that had long informed its drive for the vote was diminished, some feared, in the course of attaining its own political success.

The sixth "bill of rights" on my list is actually called a bill of rights by someone far more important than a mere academic like myself. In the early 1940s, faced with an incomplete recovery from the Great Depression and the largest war in mankind's history, Franklin D. Roosevelt promulgated an economic bill of rights that was to alter the way many of us think about government. Very deliberate in his attempts to evoke memories of the nation's founding, Roosevelt modeled his call for a new type of economic rights—decent housing, jobs, a minimum wage—on the original Bill of Rights.

We tend to forget today that Roosevelt's decision to declare an economic bill of rights was not one that he arrived at early or easily, but a difficult option largely forced upon him by economic and international conditions. Roosevelt came into office, of course, at the depth of the worst economic collapse the nation has ever experienced. Investments had plummeted after Black Monday in 1929 and continued to fall during the early 1930s. The gross national product dropped by a third, construction by three-quarters, and unemployment rates exceeded 25 percent. Large cities were among the areas hit hardest. In 1932 almost 48 percent of the work force in New York was unemployed; Chicago and other metropolises had comparable figures. Banks large and small failed, wiping out the assets of owners and investors alike. Also hard hit were farmers. As the markets for agricultural commodities collapsed, thousands of farm families were forced off the land. According to Roosevelt's famous thumbnail sketch of the situation, one-third of the nation was "ill-housed, ill-clad, and ill-nourished."[13]

President Herbert Hoover, in office less than a year when the stock market crashed in 1929, was blamed for the depression and lambasted for doing little to alleviate it. A devotee of classical economic theory, Hoover—in spite of the unprecedented economic displacement and human suffering caused by the depression—followed a traditional tight-money policy, calling upon the private sector to right itself and decrying those who advocated increased governmental spending as profligates. In 1932 the American people turned to Franklin Roosevelt, not because he promised to do anything in particular about the grave situation, but because he promised to do *something*.

Indeed, Hoover was correct in characterizing the Roosevelt of the 1932 campaign as a political chameleon. Attacking Hoover from both the left and the right, the Democrat chided the incumbent for doing little about the economic situation and, at the same time, for taking the budget out of balance. Roosevelt was able to get away with this political gimmick be-

---

[13] Quoted in Herbert D. Rosenbaum and Elizabeth Bartelme, eds., *Franklin D. Roosevelt: The Man, The Myth, The Era, 1882–1945* (New York: Greenwood Press, 1987), 85.

cause even though he promised to rebalance the budget, his rhetoric and demeanor suggested he would take firm and affirmative action on the economic front.

Roosevelt's first term in office was a vast experiment to determine what kind of economic action should be undertaken. Since he had surrounded himself with a distinguished and diverse brain trust, Roosevelt was not at a loss for ideas. Among his advisers were isolation-minded nationalists and Wilsonian internationalists; collectivists and trust-busters; inveterate planners and cantankerous individualists; business regulators, business subsidizers, and business atomizers; and balanced budgeters and deficit spenders. The whole economic panoply was represented, and Roosevelt listened to them all and without long committing himself to any course except the most expedient policy for the given moment. Although flexible and agile—both intellectually and politically—he still thought of the depression in classical economic terms and tried to address it through a series of stopgap governmental regulatory programs. Although he came to realize the necessity for a larger federal role in the economy in the early 1930s, he still clung to the sanctity of the balanced budget and had yet to grasp the fundamentals of the new economic reality.

During his first term in office Roosevelt and his brain trust designed, drafted, and pushed through Congress a series of laws designed to give the federal government more power to ease the effects of the depression. The Federal Emergency Relief Administration targeted cities for welfare and unemployment assistance. The Civil Works Administration and then the Public Works Administration and Works Progress Administration constituted job programs to give the unemployed work on public projects. The Agricultural Adjustment Act was passed, increasing farmers' buying power and decreasing debt pressures. And the National Recovery Administration was established to promote industrial recovery and fair business practice. Although such measures sailed through Congress and were popular with the public, most were quickly struck by the Supreme Court as unconstitutional. Extremely deferential to business interests, a conservative majority on the Court found much of the New Deal legislation too intrusive into what it perceived as the private economic sector.

It has intrigued many historians and biographers why, in the face of the great economic collapse and the Supreme Court's opposition to his regulatory proposals, Roosevelt did not embrace the economic philosophy of John Maynard Keynes earlier or more closely. The versatile Lord Keynes— Oxford don, entrepreneur, confidant of the powerful, speculator, member of the Bloomsbury group—had since 1919 enjoyed rankling the established academic order with radical theories on economics and public fiscal policy. He questioned the wisdom of classical economic cyclical spending, arguing that nations could better work their way out of depressions through aggressive policies of countercyclical governmental spending, fueling the demand-side of the economy with tax cuts, a looser money supply, and increased government spending.

Despite the popularity of Keynes's theory in liberal economic circles, the considerable personal correspondence between Keynes and Roosevelt, and the publication in 1936 of the magnum opus *The General Theory of Employment, Interest and Money,* the president failed to grasp the critical insights Keynes offered. With its emphasis on governmental spending rather than regulation, Keynesian policies had their advantages—not the least of which were that they probably would have been considered constitutional by the Court and would have appealed to many congressmen (who have always preferred spending to taxing). In a sense, they represented a true middle way between the equally unpopular options of laissez-faire capitalism and socialism. Roosevelt, however, found them unappealing for a number of reasons.

First, he remained committed, in the long term at least, to a balanced budget. Under continuous pressure from the right to be fiscally responsible, Roosevelt was looking for ways to cut spending as late as 1940. Second, none of his closest White House advisers was a Keynesian. Even the liberal economists in the brain trust had failed to recognize Keynes's intellectual breakthrough and like most other liberal economists remained dubious of a general countercyclical orientation. While some deficits might be necessary and pump priming might occasionally be desirable, an entire countercyclical economic plan remained a horse of an altogether different color. Third, for Roosevelt, the practical politician who liked to deal in concrete reality, Keynes's theories were far too abstruse and counterintuitive. The notion of attaining prosperity through the purposeful accumulation of large debts seemed to Roosevelt merely another fuzzy academic theory, of which he had already had his fill from numerous unsolicited sources. Finally, a Keynesian countercyclical economic policy requires commitment and dogged determination. Followed only halfheartedly, it cannot achieve growth, but will merely antagonize the business community with the size of its debt. Had Roosevelt opted for a Keynesian approach, he would have had to have done so without reservation. Even by the late 1930s, Roosevelt had not arrived at the stage where he was willing to make such a commitment. Still clinging to old economic definitions and beliefs, and caught up in the tactical exigencies of hundreds of pressing problems, Roosevelt was not about to commit himself wholeheartedly to Keynesianism and thus was unable to take advantage of the great intellectual opportunity Keynes offered.

If the depression itself failed to transform Roosevelt's economic thought, domestic politics and international affairs had a sharper impact on FDR's economics. In the 1940 election, Roosevelt faced his toughest opposition to date. Wendell Willkie—an intelligent, charming, liberal Republican utilities magnate—pressed the president hard during the campaign. A strong advocate of civil rights and America's international position, Willkie was critical of many New Deal policies as being overly restrictive on business and tried—with some success—to portray himself as the hardworking, average American businessman swamped by big government. Although Roosevelt eventually won reelection by over five million popular votes, he lost support in almost every major population category from his 1936 peak. The only categories in which support for Roosevelt remained as high in 1940 as it had previously were the lower and lower-middle socioeconomic classes. The beleaguered masses had remained loyal in the president's hour of greatest political need; he would not forget them in his third term.

Internationally in the early 1940s, much of the world was at war. The United States had entered the conflict first as an ally to belligerents; the attack on Pearl Harbor in December 1941 made it a principal. Intellectually, this posed a problem for Roosevelt and the rest of the allied world. Facing in Hitler, Mussolini, and Tojo skilled adversaries who had their own definitions of freedom that many people found compelling, Americans and others increasingly began to ask what it was they were fighting for. Not satisfied merely with fighting against something evil or for a return to prewar conditions, the men and women making tremendous sacrifices for the allies yearned for an articulation of their cause, for a compelling rationale.

Conscious of his political debt to lower-income voters and the necessities of international conflict, Roosevelt responded with a stunning new definition of liberty and the rights of citizens. As early as July 1940, during a press conference in which he was asked to delineate his objectives for a postwar world, Roosevelt had begun to articulate a new list of key freedoms. In addition to the accepted freedoms of speech and religion, he added two "freedoms from"—freedom from fear and freedom from want. These are significant, of course, because they are positive freedoms that require instead of prohibit government action. Not only must government be proscribed from infringing on speech or religious practices, but in addition it must take positive action to ensure for its citizens security and at least the basic necessities of life. In January of the following year, during his annual address to Congress, Roosevelt fleshed out the argument he had made the previous July in an economic bill of rights included in his famous "Four Freedoms." He called for "economic understandings which will secure to every nation a healthy peace time life for its inhabitants—everywhere in the world." This economic bill of rights included a call for equal opportunity, jobs for all able to work, economic security, expanded civil liberties, decreased privileges for the few, and a constantly rising standard of living. A radical departure from earlier American conceptions of the role of the state in the private lives of citizens, Roosevelt's economic bill of rights committed the public sector to taking increasing interest in and responsibility for the economic health of its citizenry. This, he said, "is no vision of a distant millennium. It is a definite basis for a kind of world attainable in our own time and generation."[14]

Roosevelt's intellectual journey during the 1930s from economic experimentation to his acceptance of the need for a systematically larger role for the government in the economy radically altered the nature of the American state. It represented a milestone on the American journey from liberal individualism to the kind of mixed economy required in the twentieth century. More than that, however, the harsh instructor Experience had provided for Roosevelt the key insight that intelligence alone had not: "necessitous men are not free men." In coming to realize and admit that true freedom demands a certain economic base, Roosevelt redefined the term liberty and altered the course of postwar American domestic policy.

The seventh and final "bill of rights" on my list pertains to the social sphere. As we associate the economic "bill of rights" with a great New Yorker, the social "bill of rights" is inseparable in our minds from the Texan whose Great Society

[14]Quoted in Commager, *Documents of American History*, 2:634.

promulgated and promoted programs designed to enhance the social conditions of millions of Americans.

To those of us who were politically active in the Democratic Party in the 1950s, Lyndon B. Johnson's eventual championing of liberal social causes still seems a bit uncharacteristic. LBJ appeared during the 1950s to be the consummate Senate man, a Southern power broker of the old school. He had come up through the ranks of Texas politics, ably representing first a conservative, rural district and later the entire state. In the Congress, he had opposed or worked to dilute many of the visionary programs first proposed by the likes of Adlai Stevenson, Hubert Humphrey, Estes Kefauver, and other members of the Democrats' left flank. In 1948, while in the House, Johnson labeled the civil rights movement "a farce and a sham—an effort to set up a police state in the guise of liberty."[15] During the 1940s and 1950s, he had repeatedly voted against bills to outlaw poll taxes and to establish a Fair Employment Practices Commission.

As Senate majority leader from 1954 to 1960, Johnson had vigorously asserted the prerogatives of that consensus-minded, centrist institution, eagerly cutting deals to dull the blades or parry the thrusts of liberal proposals. For example, he did not support any civil rights measure until 1957, when he ultimately voted in favor of a voting rights bill after having led the effort to strike its provision giving the attorney general the authority to initiate civil rights lawsuits. In short, Johnson the Senate man had been the ultimate transactional leader, operating effectively in, but never rising above, the exigencies of the political environment. Although he had been instrumental in steering a number of compromise civil rights bills through the conservative Senate, they had nearly exhausted his transactional skills and, in the final analysis, had only marginal influences on the conditions of the country's black

[15] Quoted in Ronnie Dugger, *The Politician: The Life and Times of Lyndon Johnson* (New York: W. W. Norton and Co., 1982), 310.

population. To some of us in the Democratic Party, Johnson represented the past, the old guard of the party whose ideas were antiquated and who were incapable of providing the type of positive leadership we needed to take the party and the country into the brave new world of the 1960s. When we heard, on the floor of the 1960 convention, that Jack Kennedy had chosen Johnson as his running mate, we were disappointed, and there was some talk of a liberal revolt. Johnson could not be trusted, we thought; he would only use the vice presidency to subvert, alter, or delay the Kennedy agenda. The liberal victory that seemed at hand with Kennedy's narrowly approved nomination now appeared gravely threatened.

That great teacher Clio has of course shown us how incorrect our perceptions were. We radically underestimated Johnson and the intellectual changes he would make during his move from the Senate chamber to the Oval Office. Perhaps one mistake critics made in evaluating Johnson was to overlook the profound impact his developmental years had on his adult world view. Although *Life* magazine estimated his assets at approximately fourteen million dollars in 1964, Johnson was not to the manor born.[16] The first child of civic-minded parents in east Texas, the young Johnson often had more spiritual than material sustenance. His father, an active state legislator, was forced into bankruptcy three times; members of the family wore homemade clothes and could only rarely afford meat for the dinner table; and there were periods of severe deprivation, when even ordinary necessities were sometimes beyond the family's reach. After graduating from high school at age fifteen and despite his mother's protestations that he go directly to college, Johnson headed to California looking for work. Employed intermittently for two years as a fruit picker, dishwasher, and waiter, the future president lived as a transient, from day to day, from hand to mouth.

[16] Cited in James David Barber, *The Presidential Character* (Englewood Cliffs, N.J.: Prentice-Hall, 1985), 113.

Johnson returned to Texas, attended Southwest Texas State Teachers College, and began his rise to state and national prominence. But behind the bravado expected of Texas politicians, he never forgot his upbringing: the hard times, the scrimping and saving, the menial tasks, the caprice of economic fortune, the vulnerability of individual lives to societal circumstances. When he ultimately gained a position of national influence, he used much of his considerable leadership skills to alleviate for others the conditions he himself had to overcome.

Johnson assumed the office of president under tragic yet auspicious circumstances. The assassination of the young and vibrant John F. Kennedy made a martyr of the fallen president and crusades of his causes. Johnson brought to the Oval Office not only a longstanding—albeit often well-hidden—commitment to their substance, but also considerable transformative leadership skills that many did not see at the time but that enabled him to guide proposals smoothly through to the policy stage.

Immediately upon assuming office, Johnson began to change. I have remarked elsewhere that America has a four-party rather than a two-party system. Johnson's personal transformation in the days after Kennedy's assassination took him from the ranks of the conservative "congressional Democrats" of Sam Rayburn, the Louisiana Longs, and Strom Thurmond into the tradition of the more progressive, more active, more liberal "presidential Democrats" such as Roosevelt, Truman, Stevenson, and Kennedy. He lost no time in the waning days of 1963 in salvaging what he could of the Kennedy agenda and strengthening those elements of it that he thought could be expanded. Armed with his personal experiences of deprivation, the agenda originally put in place by Kennedy, an impressive arsenal of presidential powers, and his own well-honed legislative skills, Johnson immediately went to work on an extensive series of civil rights bills. In 1964 he pushed through Congress the first substantial Civil

Rights Act, a strengthened version of the one originally proposed by Kennedy the preceding year. The president actively
managed the bill's journey through the legislative process, especially in using his personal influence to break a Senate fili-
buster that threatened to scuttle the Act. In explaining why
certain provisions of the Act—especially those relating to the
use of public facilities by blacks—were necessary, Johnson
perhaps recalled his own family's struggles when he argued
that "a man has a right not to be insulted in public in front of
his children."[17]

The Civil Rights Act of 1964 was followed by a veritable
avalanche of subsequent social legislation, making the mid-
1960s the most fertile legislative period since Roosevelt's fa-
bled "One Hundred Days," in 1933, or his "Second Hundred
Days," in 1935. The theme for his vision of America was
sounded by Johnson during a speech at the University of
Michigan, on May 22, 1964. "The Great Society," he said,
"rests on abundance and liberty for all. It demands an end to
poverty and racial injustice, to which we are totally committed in our time. But that is just the beginning."[18] Arguing
that Americans were morally bound to use their abundance to
create this Great Society that would benefit all citizens, particularly the least advantaged, Johnson succeeded in persuad-
ing Congress to pass legislation funding Medicare, increasing
aid to education on all levels, creating a number of extensive
antipoverty programs, giving teeth to civil rights guarantees
through the 1965 Voting Rights Act, and aiding the nation's
ailing cities through creation of the Department of Housing
and Urban Development. Johnson's tireless efforts, his de-
cisiveness, his excellent staff, and his famed "treatment" made
him as effective as any president of the twentieth century.

The impact of Johnson's leadership during the turbulent

[17] Quoted in George F. Will, *Statecraft as Soulcraft: What Government Does*
(New York: Simon and Schuster, 1983), 87.

[18] Quoted in Eric F. Goldman, *The Tragedy of Lyndon Johnson* (New York: Alfred A. Knopf, 1969), 166.

1960s may best be evaluated by what happened after the height of the Great Society efforts. Despite Johnson's fall from grace over the debacle in Vietnam and the reorientation of the country along a more conservative axis with the election of Richard Nixon in 1968, the basic assumptions of the Great Society have remained largely unshaken. In the areas of civil rights, welfare, health care, education, and others, a fundamentally larger role for the federal government has become accepted by liberals, moderates, and many conservatives. The federal government is still seen as the legitimate guarantor of political participation, civil rights, a minimal standard of living, social stability, and—although this sounds grandiose—human dignity. Even subsequent politicians whose rhetoric has denounced the liberality of the Great Society have through their actions recognized that the clock cannot be turned back and that the transformations accomplished by the social bill of rights have irrevocably altered American democracy.

What Johnson learned during his hard upbringing in east Texas and what he did not forget during his ascendance to the presidency was that abstract rights mean little in the face of debilitating social conditions that preclude their exercise. These adverse social conditions have many dimensions, are not merely economic, and require a concentrated and coordinated national commitment if they are to be overcome. While Johnson did not succeed in eliminating the many social conditions that impinge upon freedom, his efforts certainly worked to limit their impacts. And the social "bill of rights" to which Johnson committed the nation has expanded the democratic process by alleviating many of the social impediments to meaningful public participation.

While these are the "bills of rights" that have reached fruition to date, other significant developments may force an early revision of this list. Let me suggest a few of the areas in which substantial strides are being made and that might be candidates for inclusion on a future list. First, in the years since the

Supreme Court's famous 1965 *Griswold* decision, in which it ruled that states could not outlaw contraceptives, there has been a growing social concern over privacy. As the world becomes more crowded, more noisy, and increasingly urbanized, the protection of privacy—from intrusion by governments, corporations, communities, and our fellow citizens—may become a very high priority. Second, the rights of children have recently received considerable interest. If we as a nation are to take equality of opportunity seriously, we will simply have to do more to provide resources to underprivileged children. A great, largely untapped, resource is squandered every year as millions of children still lack even minimal opportunities to develop their talents and fulfill their potential. A larger social role is needed, it would seem, to guarantee children basic rights of opportunity.

Third, there is a burgeoning movement for a cultural "bill of rights." In the next decade or two there will be creative efforts undertaken to define the proper sphere of liberties to be enjoyed by teachers, performing artists, visual artists, writers, scholars, journalists, critics, and others similarly engaged in cultural pursuits. Again, this will involve not only governmental action, but community pressure, corporate responsibilities, and the extent of permissible judicial interference. Finally, there is in the land an increasing interest in community rights. Some feel we have pushed individualism too far, to the point of atomism, and that we need to reinvigorate our communal spirit. Recent works such as the acclaimed *Habits of the Heart* have stressed themes of commitment and the need for a return to more communitarian values. Perhaps an older notion of rights as invested in certain corporations, such as the community, will emerge in America. What we can be sure of, however, is that American interest in and commitment to rights as an essential element of democratic politics have not spent themselves and will not soon fade.

This brings us to the end of my survey of America's "bills of rights." I believe their history provides us with two important lessons. First, the fact that they have all been incorporated, formally or informally, into our political order suggests that our constitutional system is flexible enough to balance the twin dictates of individual rights and majority rule. We have revitalized an eighteenth-century, "horse-and-buggy" institutional and procedural constitutional order with dynamic, evolving, nineteenth- and twentieth-century "bills of rights." Almost one hundred and fifty years ago, Tocqueville wrote of the irresistible march of democracy and the growth of egalitarianism in the western world's political culture. The expansion of political participation under the "bills of rights" proves that the American regime has been able to accommodate an increasingly democratic system without a loss of political or personal liberty. Given what we know of world history, that is no mean feat.

But a second lesson is that perhaps our system, with its plethora of checks and balances, allows of such changes too sparingly. Our veto-ridden system required the agony of a civil war to push it toward emancipation, one hundred years of acrimonious agitation to compel it—begrudgingly—to grant even the most fundamental political rights to women, and the worst economic collapse in history to convince it of the need for a more positive role for the national government. We were fortunate in the past to have been able to afford the "luxuries" of such slow action and the appeasement of those minority elements that sought—through various manipulations of the system—to contain or deflect the movement of popular democracy. I am not sure we will continue to be able to afford such extravagancies in the future, as the time frame available for action decreases in the face of ever-accumulating technology and the escalating pace of international affairs. It is clear to me that our commitment to individual rights can place tremendous strains on our institutional structures. Rights often raise expectations about government that institutions may be systematically incapable of fulfilling.

While I advocate no rash or ill-considered reforms, in this

year of constitutional commemoration we would be wise indeed to begin a public discourse on the adequacy of our existing institutions for the tumultuous decades that lie ahead. If
they cannot peacefully integrate and accommodate the legitimate demands of newly defined groups—immigrants, the
aged, homosexuals, and many others—perhaps our institutions are in need of some measure of constitutional reform.
As in the past, we will need intellectual and imaginative
leadership of an extremely high caliber to guide our constitutional surrey in the years to come. A critical public cerebration
on the Constitution in this, its two hundredth year, could
only serve to guide and inform such leaders.

In the pages that follow, I will deal in greater detail with the
intricacies associated with our attempted balance of majority
rule within a constitutional order. First, I will explore the odd
notion of representation, examine several alternative types of
representation, and consider what prospects they offer for
improving our existing order. Then, in conclusion, I will outline some of my own recommendations for concomitantly expanding majoritarianism and individual rights in our system.

CHAPTER 3

RIGHTS, RULE, AND REPRESENTATION: A CRITIQUE OF REPRESENTATIVE ARRANGEMENTS

TO RECAPITULATE, the problem as I have couched it is that there is, in theory at least, a profound tension between two values we hold dear: majority rule and minority rights. Over the course of most of American history, this tension has remained merely theoretical, as our political culture and the circumstances of history bought time for our inefficient political institutions to expand both individual and group freedoms and democratic rule simultaneously. More recently, however, that has not been as easily accomplished. Increasingly, it seems, demands for new rights cannot be easily correlated in our system with the necessity for efficient, majority rule; in essence, we are finding it harder to balance minority rights with those of the majority. In our technologically and socially advanced age, when most interest groups are well organized and politically savvy, when scientific advances—many carrying important social ramifications—come with dizzying speed, when a changing international order presses new problems upon us almost daily, such a problem is a serious one.

In thinking about this problem, it is instructive to notice that it has two primary dimensions, one intellectual, the other decidedly more practical. After addressing the first of these dimensions rather summarily, I will concentrate on the practical side of the problem.

Intellectually, the problem as posed demands that we have

63

some guidelines for determining which demands of the minorities and the majority are legitimate and which are not. We need some measuring stick to judge where the critical balance should be established. While an exhaustive treatment of this issue is far beyond the scope of my purposes here, it seems to me that the history of political thought has provided a useful—if not wholly satisfying—answer in the distinction between the noble versus the perverted state. This concept originated with the ancient Greeks and focuses not on who rules, but rather on how well they rule, or even on their motivations for ruling.

In *The Politics*, Aristotle, for instance, distinguished between kingship (rule of the single just man) and tyranny (rule of one man seeking his own advantage); aristocracy (rule by the best citizens) and oligarchy (rule by the self-interested wealthy); and timocracy (rule by civic-minded property owners) and democracy (rule by the avaricious masses).[1] Later, Polybius, the Greek historian of ancient Rome, similarly distinguished between democracy and ochlocarcy. A society was democratic in his scheme only when it was ruled by the majority of its citizens acting in a considered, thoughtful manner. If, on the other hand, the citizens exercised their will in an arbitrary or capricious manner, they were said to be ochlocartic.[2] Such distinctions occur repeatedly in ancient political theory and revolve around the central concept of social responsibility. Those systems that encouraged rule by socially responsible agents were considered noble; those that did not, which permitted governance by parties interested principally in their own profit, were labeled as corrupt. Many of the ancients employed a vocabulary that considered democratic only those polities that were ruled by a responsible majority.

In a sense, this distinction has been retained through much

---

[1] Aristotle, *The Politics*, trans. T. A. Sinclair (New York: Penguin Books, 1962), 186–90.

[2] Polybius, *The Histories*, trans. W. R. Paton (London: Heinemann, 1922–1927), 6 vols.

of western political thought and certainly informs the American tradition, where it is reflected in the founders' profound apprehension of factions. While the founders believed that only popular rule could be just, they were—as we have seen—suspicious of possible majority factions and unwilling to hand the reins of government over to a seething rabble. According to the old adage by Madison, even "[h]ad every Athenian citizen been a Socrates, every Athenian assembly would still have been a mob."[3]

For the founders, a way out of this problem—how to create a noble, rather than a corrupt, form of popular government—lay in representation. Conceptually, at least, it provided a way for the people to retain ultimate sovereignty, while removing from their mercurial temperaments responsibility for the day-to-day operation of government. Consequently, not a mob, but the reflective representatives of the people, would govern.

Unlike democracy, the idea of representation, while not unknown to the ancient Greeks, is in practice a fairly modern notion. Thomas Hobbes, in 1650, referred to representation in *Leviathan*,[4] and John Locke discussed the term at great length in his *The Second Treatise of Government*, in 1692.[5] Largely because of this, representation is linked very strongly in our minds with the liberal tradition. As the societal consensus that had provided the basis for political unity since the time of the ancients began to disintegrate under the strains of the massive technological, political, economic, and religious advances of the postmedieval world, more heterogeneous societies developed that contained powerful, disparate interests. As the political theorists of that day strove to find ways of harnessing these interests and taming them, they hit upon the notion of representation. The striving, yearning, unruly

---

[3] Hamilton, Jay, and Madison, *The Federalist* (see chap. 1, n. 6), 361.

[4] Thomas Hobbes, *Leviathan*, ed. Michael Oakshott (New York: Collier Books, 1962).

[5] John Locke, *The Second Treatise of Government*, ed. Thomas A. Peardon (Indianapolis: Bobbs-Merrill Educational Publishing, 1952).

interests that constituted a society would be represented in some fashion, in some forum, where decisions would be made by the respective representatives concerning how the society would be structured and operated. Liberal theoreticians realized they could not recreate the old social consensus, that spirit having been loosed and dissipated by the Pandora of modernity, but they hoped that some type of representative scheme could provide at least enough social cohesion to allow for the peaceful pursuit of the people's various individual interests.

At the heart of the notion of representation, in any form, lies the suspicion that the people themselves may not always—or even often—be able to articulate what is in their best interests. They may be unable to perceive their interest; they may be unskilled at promoting their interest; they may surrender their interests to corrupt office holders or demagogues. Even more, they may be unable to weigh properly the competing claims of short-term versus long-term interests; or they may but poorly realize how, in a social environment, their interests must be balanced against those of others. For whatever the reason, representational theory assumes that we may not necessarily know how best to represent ourselves.

This suspicion is nicely encapsulated in the old judicial saw about the lawyer who, in representing himself, has a fool for a client. Notice the wisdom in this old saying. It is not the lawyer qua lawyer who is the fool, but the lawyer qua client. Those who try to represent themselves are simply too close to their cases, so close that they will not only be incapable of seeing what is in their own best interest, but will be blind to the larger needs of the system, as well. We must remember that lawyers are not merely representatives of and counselors for their clients, but are also officers of the court, charged not only with operating within the system, but doing what they can to protect it. Principals in legal actions are often so consumed with the outcome of their cases that they ignore the larger institutional and procedural issues on which the entire legal system rests. Lawyers, representative of both their clients and the court, cannot afford to become so consumed. In my mind, this odd dual allegiance is true of all good representatives.

James Madison, who more than anyone else can be said to be the intellectual architect of our American constitutional system, clearly perceived this duality. Writing in *Federalist* 10, he argued that "the delegation of the government . . . to a small number of citizens elected by the rest . . . [serves] to refine and enlarge the public views, by passing them through the medium of a chosen body of citizens, whose wisdom may best discern the true interest of their country, and whose patriotism and love of justice will be least likely to sacrifice it to temporary or partial considerations." The public voice, Madison contended, will be "more consonant to the public good" when spoken through representatives "than if pronounced by the people themselves."[6]

If, intellectually, we accept Madison's reasoning that representation provides the basis for a superior form of democracy, we are still faced with the practical problem: what type of representational system adequately balances the legitimate claims of private constituents with the legitimate dictates of public concern? Or, as we have been phrasing it, what type of representation can best guarantee both minority rights and majority rule within a stable political order?

It is a question that has puzzled students of democracy for centuries, prompting them to develop elaborate theories, political structures, and voting schemes designed to ensure the election of "good" representatives. The American system of electing legislators from single-member districts is merely one of a number of competing types of representation to be found in the world. Whether or not it contributes to the election of sufficiently talented and disinterested representatives re-

6 Hamilton, Jay, and Madison, *The Federalist,* 59.

mains open to debate, but enough doubt remains in many people's minds as to produce periodic calls for the United States to scrap this system and adopt another one.

In this year of Constitutional reflection, I do not think it wise to dismiss such ideas out of hand. Indeed, in the spirit of the founders, we should at least be willing to entertain the possibility that the founders made a serious mistake, giving us a badly flawed type of representation, and that we might be well served to choose some other manner of representation as the cornerstone for our national government. To make such decisions, we need to examine in some detail the other candidates. What other varieties of representation are there; what advantages do they offer; what liabilities do they carry; are there any clearly superior, realistic alternatives to our present system? At best, an exploration of such questions might yield viable options for change; at worst, it cannot but illuminate the problem and, perhaps, suggest ways in which our present system might be reformed if it cannot be replaced.

Let us begin with the two basic varieties of representation, and let us call these formal and informal. Informal representation is that accomplished without the specific consent of those being represented. It is representation in the same sense in which a parent represents the interest of a minor child or an absolute monarch represents the interests of his realm. What the king or the parent represents are certain fundamental continuities and heritages. In the monarchical case, it is the nation's tradition, its status, its standing that the regent represents. The consent of the people is neither requested nor given, and the relative stations of the parties involved are such as to make it inappropriate. Since the power and authority involved in such relationships reside in the representative and not the represented, the character of the king or the parent is of the utmost concern. With few constraints imposed upon them by their children or their subjects, who lack anything like a recall vote as it were, only the representatives' sense of duty to their people provides any brake to their caprice.

Human history has tragically shown, however, that such restraints are often tenuous and the presence of virtuous monarchs all too rare. As Madison noticed in *Federalist* 10, it is risky to count on the presence of enlightened rulers to provide skilled leadership, because "[e]nlightened statesmen will not always be at the helm."[7] This type of "informal" representation, absent a just and loving parent or an enlightened prince, is a perilous proposition. Capable of ignoring the needs and legitimate desires of the people, autocrats often do so. The result is a style of governance that caters not to the people or the nation, but to the interests, convenience, and preferences of the ruler. Formal representation, on the other hand, entails some sort of consent by the represented. Through some mechanism, by some formula, there is an explicit agreement between the governed and the governors, where the governors rule at the pleasure of the governed.

In its simplest form, formal representation is plebiscitary. At large meetings, citizens come together to inform their governors of their preferences. I do not need to speak remotely of this type of representation because I live in New England, where town meetings are the official governing organs of 88 percent of the municipalities in the region. As an active citizen, I have been all too involved in this type of government in my hometown of Williamstown. I will admit that I am not nearly the uncritical partisan of town meetings that some keen observers of America, such as Tocqueville and Lord Bryce, have been. They tend to make for very long and dreary evenings, during which every member of the community has—and many exercise—the right to stand up and speak, often at length. Since the meeting season occurs in the spring, during the basketball and hockey playoffs, attendance is often

[7] Ibid., 57.

very low, with 5 percent of registered voters being considered a good turnout. In addition, most of those who do come do not stay for the entire session. By the end of the evening, usually only diehards, not necessarily including myself, remain, casting rather severe doubts on whether those present are in any way representative of the citizenry.

In my many years of attending such meetings, I have come to notice several curious phenomena. For one thing, while large appropriation proposals often sail through with little or no discussion or argument, such meetings often tend to mire down on fairly small details. Immediately after approving a three-quarters of a million dollar item in a little more than a heartbeat, for instance, a town meeting might enter an acrimonious debate over the need for a $12,000 truck for park maintenance. Moreover, tangential but emotive issues have begun to emerge in such meetings, tending to divert and discredit the entire process. In recent years, for example, town meetings all over the region have taken to venting their opinions on such national issues as abortion, the nuclear freeze, and the federal deficit. In the view of many critics, this not only diverts attention away from more substantive items on the agenda, but, in the words of one observer, contributes to a "circuslike atmosphere." Finally, as municipal affairs have become more extensive and complicated, town meetings have become increasingly vulnerable to private special interests and public technocrats. These individuals not only are able to pack public meetings, but also to control agendas effectively so as to make the issues incomprehensible to the average citizen, who attends only one or two such meetings a year. Partly as a result of these developments, some expect that the town meeting may over time become considerably less popular as a form of municipal government, with towns across the region considering switching to mayoral and council arrangements.

Plebiscitary representation occurs on larger scales as well, often in state-level referenda that have become quite popular in many places. This year there were twenty-seven "initiatives" and other forms of referenda on the state ballot in Texas. Issues addressed in these initiatives ranged from pari-mutuel betting to municipal liability, to toll-road bonds, to a proposed super collider; all of them passed. California, which has become famous or infamous for its "propositions," also often has dozens of issues on its ballots that citizens decide by direct vote. In 1986 state citizens voted on propositions related to safe drinking water, the election of district attorneys, English as the official state language, and restrictions on toxic substances. Do the citizens of these states have a great feeling of power, directly deciding such a wide variety of issues that affect them? Do they feel themselves uniquely in control of their political destinies? Do they feel their interests are better represented when they are not filtered through the normal legislative process? From my experience, the answer to all these questions is an emphatic no. Most voters do not feel more efficacious, but less; they do not feel in control, but impotent. Keeping informed on the many, often abstruse issues is time-consuming and difficult. Many citizens, I think, do not make the effort and therefore feel overwhelmed when asked to cast such votes, forced to decide among alternatives they lack the information to evaluate properly.

What is more, referenda in many instances do not actually allow citizens to decide policy, but merely to voice their aspirations on certain issues. The nuclear-freeze referenda that passed in nine states in the early 1980s did not make American strategic policy; that is forbidden to the states under our federal system. All they allowed was the articulation of a public frustration with the vagaries of our nuclear posturing. While that may have been a noble goal, the use of referenda to achieve such purposes seems to cheapen the democratic process. The people ostensibly are given a voice, but in practice it is a political sleight of hand; referendum or not, they have no say in policy.

A second species of formal representation includes various types of parliamentary schemes. We will discuss three of the

types here: single-member pluralities, multimember pluralities, and proportional representation.

The single-member district variety is the classic example of
the parliamentary system. It is the type of representation
used in the mother of legislatures, the British Parliament, and
the United States House of Representatives. Under this system, as the name suggests, the country is divided into geographical districts, each of which elects one representative. In
any given election, the candidate who wins the plurality of
the votes cast—or, in British parlance, is the "first past the
post"—is the representative for that constituency. There is
no reward for finishing second except for the party's feeble
thanks for carrying its standard. The principal virtue of a
single-member district arrangement is that it contributes to
the propagation of a stable two-party system. A single-member
district provides little hope and few incentives for an unknown political candidate or a new, small party. Quite the opposite, the incentive structure in such a political arrangement
provides considerable impetus for such actors to join one of
the two major parties and work within it for their political objectives. It is no accident that Great Britain and the United
States, two countries that employ single-member districts extensively (though not exclusively), have also experienced
stable, two-party rule for much of their histories.

Single-member district arrangements also have a downside,
however, in that they tend to underrepresent minorities
while overrepresenting majorities. This relates to what is
commonly referred to as the "cube law" of politics. While this
is not the place to discuss the intricacies nor debate the preci-
sion of that term, we should note that if national minorities
are evenly spread over constituencies, they will also usually
be local minorities. As such, they will tend to be underrepre-
sented in single-member systems since in each contest they
can consistently be outvoted by the local majority. That has,
unfortunately, been the experience of such nationally distributed minorities as Indians in Malaysia and blacks in the

United States. It has not been at all uncommon to find such minorities having nowhere near the level of representation their proportion of the population would suggest. Even in instances of completely unbiased districting—that is, in the absence of gerrymandering—minorities may experience gross underrepresentation due to the mechanics of single-member elections. As a result, American blacks and Hispanics who form 11 and 9 percent of the population, respectively, usually garner far fewer congressional seats: 3 1/2 and 1 percent, respectively.

Perhaps the most topical example of this phenomenon is a British one. Emerging in the early 1980s as a challenger to the old Conservative and Labour parties, the Social Democrat–Liberal Alliance sought to capitalize on its large middle-class following. Although it has nearly matched the Labour Party's aggregate popular vote, its voters are so evenly diffused across the country that it lacks the concentrated support in "winnable" districts required to make it competitive under Britain's "first-past-the-post" system, leaving it with very few seats in Parliament. For example, in 1983 the Alliance won 26 percent of the popular vote (to Labour's 28 percent), yet was awarded only 27 (4 percent) of the 650 seats in the House of Commons. In 1987 the results were similar, with the Alliance garnering 23 percent of the popular vote, but less than 3 1/2 percent (22) of the seats.

While not nearly as common as single-member plurality districts, multimember—or at-large—districts have been and still are used extensively in state and local elections. Such contests involve large districts that elect a number of representatives. Each voter is allowed to cast as many votes as there are seats. Designed to open the electoral process, cure the evils of local ward politics, and help integrate urban with suburban/rural districts, in effect multimember districts severely discriminate against minority voting blocs. Often, under such schemes, the majority group is able to garner all the available seats in the large district even though under a single-member arrangement the minority group might have been able to capture several of the smaller districts. Numerous studies of American state and local political systems have found that multimember plurality districts handicap minorities even more than traditional single-member plurality districts do.[8]

The other principal subspecies of parliamentary systems is proportional representation, or PR as it is often called. The logic here is exactly the reverse of that of the single-member or multimember plurality districts. Instead of a constituency electing one or more representatives on the basis of a plurality vote, it elects several, with the breakdown decided on the basis of each party's (or ethnic group's, or religious minority's) proportion of the population. While PR has diverse manifestations (for example, party list, single transferable vote), all have the same rationale: the election of representatives who reflect better the demographic characteristics and political proportions of the population. It offers substantial advantages to minorities because they do not have to constitute a majority in any district to be able to elect representatives to the legislature. It could be called minorities rule.

PR has enjoyed the endorsement of some noted political theorists (including John Stuart Mill, who termed it "among the very greatest improvements yet made in the theory and practice of government"[9]) and has been employed in a number of different countries. In instances where it works, it tends to produce integration in divided societies. Belgium, split between the Germanic Flemings in the north and the francophone Walloons in the south, instituted a PR system in 1899. That system has been credited with contributing to the

[8] For a survey of this literature, see Bernard Grofman, "Alternatives to Single-Member Plurality Districts: Legal and Empirical Issues," in *Representation and Redistricting Issues*, ed. Bernard Grofman, et al. (Lexington, Mass.: Lexington Books, 1982), 107–28.

[9] John Stuart Mill, *Considerations on Representative Government* (New York: Forum Books, 1958), 111.

unification of the country and the transformation of the formerly language-based parties into truly national parties. Similarly, the quasi-PR system employed in West Germany is often cited as performing an integrative role between the Catholic and Protestant communities, and the Israeli PR scheme, which encourages negotiations and compromises between a variety of groups, is often credited with helping to preserve and unite the fragile social mosaic of that country.

PR, however, has problems as well. In some situations—such as when it has been attempted in Northern Ireland—it fails to promote integration and may lead to a rigidification of minority positions. Since no majority sanction is necessary, proportional representation makes it possible for a minority to elect representatives responsible to the minority alone, insulated from the will of the majority. Such minority representatives may be tempted to assume an intransigent posture vis-a-vis the majority and, in order to ensure their popularity with their minority constituent base, remain uncompromising with the majority.

Sometimes PR can result in too accurate a reflection of a society's demographics. Such was the case in New York City in the 1930s and 1940s, when a proportional representation scheme was utilized for the selection of city aldermen. Under this system, in 1945 the Communist Party was endorsed by 9 percent of the voting public and, therefore, received 9 percent (two) of the twenty-three council seats. Appalled by these results and the presence on its governing council of a cadre of Marxists, the city abandoned PR in 1947, as American relations with the Soviet Union deteriorated. There had been, so it seemed, in this experiment in representative democracy, far too much representation for the "bad guy."

Perhaps the greatest drawback to PR, however, is the factionalizing effect it can have upon a society's party system. If a "first-past-the-post" arrangement encourages a stable, two-party system, PR, by raising expectations of minority representation, provides incentives for the formation of a multitude of small parties. A typical result is a host of parliamentary parties stretching from right to left across the political spectrum. The formation of a government in such situations often depends upon the ability of a group of parties (for example, Labour and Fine Gael in Ireland, the SPD and the Free Democrats in Germany, the "government of national unity" in Israel) to form and maintain a working parliamentary coalition. Often such coalitions cannot be maintained in the face of new or divisive issues. Instead, an ideological warfare often ensues, driving the coalition partners back to their core constituents and causing the government to fall. PR can, in effect, put a hair trigger on governmental instability, which has serious consequences for the representational process. What kind of representation can occur in a turbulent political atmosphere where governments are unstable, coalitions ephemeral, and potential coalition partners forever shifting? With so many fingers on the parliamentary trigger, the political situation may explode at any time.

The most disturbing example of the pernicious effects of PR still remains the Weimar Republic. In typical German fashion, the Weimar constitution, adopted after the end of the First World War, established a gruelingly precise system of proportional representation that included a number of elaborate vote-transfer mechanisms designed to reflect, as accurately as possible, the popular partisan cleavages. The result was a kind of rabid pluralism in which five major parties and countless smaller ones engaged in a frenzied struggle for parliamentary power in the Reichstag. In the first ten years of the republic (1919–28), fifteen different cabinets governed the state; none survived for more than eighteen months, and many did not last even three. For long stretches, the government was in the hands of caretaker, minority cabinets that had to scrape together ad hoc coalitions on each issue as it emerged. The fundamental characteristic of government in the Weimar became the singular absence of any kind of sustained leadership. The Reichstag, where the parties of the center should have been able to exercise moderate and responsible leadership, became the butt of derisive jokes as coalition after coalition proved itself incapable of governance. Some scholars, such as Ferdinand A. Hermens, lay the blame squarely at the foot of the republic's PR scheme and argue that the subsequent vacuum of leadership, direction, and firmness, in concert with the worldwide economic depression, contributed to the German people's willingness to accept the horrendous alternative offered by Adolf Hitler's National Socialist Party.[10]

A third kind of formal representation is class-based representation. Under such arrangements, representation is either allotted according to class groupings or to one particular class, which assumes a key representational role for society.

The best example of the former is undoubtedly the infamous Prussian three-class system of voting. In 1849, Prussia reversed its trend toward the liberalization of suffrage and amended its constitution to employ a representational scheme based on socioeconomic classes. Under the terms of the arrangement, the population was divided into thirds based upon the distribution of the direct tax burden. The rich landowning group that paid one-third of the taxes was allowed to choose one-third of the representatives to the state legislature (the Landstat). The professional and artisan classes that paid the next one-third of the taxes also chose one-third of the representatives, as did the lower, sharecropper classes, who paid the bottom third of the taxes and chose the final one-third of the representatives. Although it could make some claim to universal male suffrage (all men twenty-five years of age and older were allowed to vote), the system distorted the popular will by weighing more heavily the preferences of the elite, Junker classes. While every man had a vote, the votes were not all of equal value.

---

[10]Ferdinand A. Hermens, *Democracy or Anarchy?: A Study of Proportional Representation* (South Bend, Ind.: University of Notre Dame Press, 1941).

Combined with an intimidatory public-ballot voting procedure, which was designed to pressure the lower classes into
voting as the upper-class employers and landowners would
have them, the result of the three-tiered voting system was to
inflate grossly the legislative power of the conservative upper
classes. On the eve of World War I, in the 1913 state elections,
the Prussian conservative parties controlled almost 50 percent
of the seats in the Landstat although they garnered only approximately 17 percent of the popular vote. Conversely, the
Social Democratic Party, which was very popular with the
lower classes, won only 2 percent of the legislative seats despite capturing almost 30 percent of the popular vote. Although the class-based system was ditched after Germany's
collapse at the end of the First World War, the skewed political power it gave to Prussian conservatives is often cited as
one of the causes for the war and Germany's protraction of its
war efforts long after it had any realistic hope for victory.

The second kind of class-based representation is one that we
are more familiar with, the reliance of the Marxists on the proletariat. In a sense, this is based on majoritarian arguments. In
the *Manifesto of the Communist Party,* Karl Marx and Friedrich
Engels contended that "[a]ll previous historical movements
were movements of minorities or in the interests of minorities.
The proletarian movement is the self-conscious, independent
movement of the immense majority, in the interests of the immense majority."[11] In other writings, it becomes obvious, however, that the unique virtue of the proletariat is not its size, but
its consciousness of its "historic task." The proletariat, in
effect, is both a product of the inhumanity of class-based society and mankind's potential for historical progress, the one
class capable of leading mankind toward a higher state of
being, toward a classless society. In an 1844 draft of *The Holy*

---

[11] Karl Marx and Friedrich Engels, *The Marx-Engels Reader*, ed. Robert C.
Tucker (New York: W. W. Norton and Co., 1978), 482.

Family: A Critique of Critical Criticism, a satirical attack on the Young Hegelians, Marx wrote:

> Since the fully formed proletariat represents, practically speaking, the completed abstraction from everything human, even from the appearance of being human; since all the living conditions of contemporary society have reached the acme of inhumanity in the living conditions of the proletariat . . . the proletariat itself can and must liberate itself. But it cannot liberate itself without destroying its own living conditions. It cannot do so without destroying all the inhuman living conditions of contemporary society which are concentrated in its own situation.[12]

This sort of revolutionary representation has both virtues and vices. There is but little question that Marx's prognosis of the demeaning position of the proletariat and its grueling existence was profound and insightful. But "was" is the operative word here. It is far from clear that Marx's prescription of a radical dictatorship of the proletariat any longer has currency. In the United States and the other western democracies, the working classes have proven to be more conservative, more variegated, and more easily assimilated into the upper classes than Marx thought likely. In other, poorer societies that have lacked the class mobility found in the West, efforts to found proletariat states have often deteriorated into tyrannical rule under various "cults of personality." In all, the hopes of the Marxists for a truly representational, radical, and revolutionary proletariat have been largely disappointed.

A fourth variety of formal representation is found in corporatism. As the name suggests, what is represented in corporatism is not the people directly, but rather the various "corporations" that together constitute a society. Dating at least from middle ages, the classical manifestation of corporatism is the medieval city-state. In these societies, craftsmen be-

---

[12] Ibid., 134.

longed to guilds, which established rules for their members and, with town officials, helped govern and manage public affairs. Thinking of themselves in an organic sense—with the city-state as the whole body of which each guild was a vital part that needed to work in harmony with the other bodily parts—the guilds sought consensus, harmony, and the systematic avoidance of conflict.

The idea of Korporationen was employed by G. W. F. Hegel, who in the *Philosophy of Right* envisioned them as a type of second family in civil society, capable of drawing man out of his personal isolation, elevating and rationalizing his existence, and correlating his economic self-interests with the larger needs of society. Corporations became, in fact, one of Hegel's two ethical roots for the state, outside of which free man cannot exist.[13]

In the twentieth century corporatism has experienced support from more sullied quarters. The national socialism that swept Germany and, especially, Italy in the 1920s and 1930s had a large corporatist component. Benito Mussolini's National Fascist Party was particularly adamant that the Italian people could be represented better by society's natural economic forces than by its frail and ineffective party system. The taint cast upon corporatism by its association with fascism has only recently begun to fade. This is partially because of corporatism's recent successes in a number of European states, and it is partially because of the academic rehabilitation of corporatist theory. As it has been practiced in such places as Sweden, Austria, Switzerland, Norway, and West Germany, neo-corporatism usually entails some sort of semi-official economic and social council where members of the state's bureaucracy meet with the sanctioned peak organizations of labor and business to make economic policies that are then rubber-stamped by the country's parliament.

[13] G. W. F. Hegel, *Philosophy of Right*, trans. T. M. Knox (London: Oxford University Press, 1952), 152–55.

The benefits of neo-corporatist arrangements, in which representation is effectively economically based, can be compelling for states whose economies are vulnerable to international forces and require considerable social cooperation to be competitive. Corporatist schemes can make an economy more flexible, decrease the time economic actors spend infighting, and maximize a society's ability to respond to international market forces. As a result, corporatist arrangements and the societies that have employed them have flourished during certain periods of the recent past. Obversely, however, there are significant problems associated with this kind of representation. In the first place, since this style of policy making largely bypasses the legislature, it is questionable how representative it is of society as a whole. While it may be representative of and beneficial to the members of the peak associations (that is, big labor and big industry) involved, there is no guarantee—and ample reason to doubt—that everyone concerned will have adequate access to the representative arena. Second, due to the inherently inferior negotiating position of organized labor in most situations, corporatism often institutionalizes the superiority of capital and results in vastly inequitable outcomes that enjoy government sanction. Interestingly, corporatism simultaneously undermines internal labor democracy by forcing the unions, if they are to have anything like the solidarity of business owners, to invest in highly authoritarian internal power structures.

Third, corporatism is inherently conservative. The corporate bodies that are involved and that are best able to profit from the system are those representing well-established interests. Although they may or may not be competitive and may lag far behind real world developments, they often have the organizational clout to demand governmental protection and to rob resources from more promising—but less well-organized—cutting-edge concerns. This can tie a society to outmoded policies and technologies. Fourth and finally, corporatism is limited by its economic myopia. While such arrangements may be capable of dealing adequately with some economic problems, that is all they are capable of doing. There are many other pressing social issues that corporatism simply has no mechanism for addressing. Unfortunately, since corporatism can also contribute to the withering away of a society's political institutions by diverting policy making resources to other arenas, it can thereby undermine a society's ability to confront and address such issues.

A fifth species of formal representation includes a variety of systems employing some sort of qualified majority. In such cases, more than a plurality or a simple majority is required to sanction a law, but a more onerous modified majority. Sometimes this majority must be very large, say, two-thirds of those voting. In other instances, concomitant majorities from designated geographical regions are required to pass a proposal. We will consider three variations on this theme.

The first is what is commonly known as a confederation, a group of autonomous and independent entities that form some common political institutions and agree to common action in some limited spheres of activity. In contrast to a federation, which stresses the sovereignty of the common, central authority, a confederation ensures the retention of sovereignty by the various constituent elements. This is buttressed by requirements that usually require either unanimity or very large majorities to pass even the most mundane of laws. Interestingly, in such arrangements, the duties of elected representatives often take on an oddly diplomatic cast. Since they owe primary allegiance to the member of the confederation that elected them—not to the confederation itself—they tend to interact with other elected officials not as collegial legislators, but as independent diplomats. Under the American Articles of Confederation, for instance, delegates to the Congress were more ambassadors than legislators, being paid directly by the states they served and subject to recall by the states at any moment.

Confederation has been championed by a number of political luminaries, who have seen in it the promise of the best of both worlds: the internal freedoms offered by the constituent small republics, as well as the international prestige and security of a large state. Montesquieu summed up this line of reasoning in Book IX of *The Spirit of the Laws* when he observed that: "[a]s [a confederation] is composed of petty republics, it enjoys the internal happiness of each; and with regard to its external situation, by means of the association, it possesses all the advantages of large monarchies."[14]

Unfortunately, in practice, confederacies have been far more unstable than Montesquieu suspected. The lack of strong central leadership, the tendency toward internal bickering among the constituent states, and the reliance on extraordinary majorities often severely hamper a confederacy's ability to respond to both domestic and foreign issues and to plan ahead. As a result, most confederations have either mutated into federations (as happened in Switzerland and the United States with the ratification of the Constitution) or have been defeated militarily by more unified nations (as was the case with both the Confederate States of America and the German Bund, which was eventually defeated from within by Prussia).

A particular kind of confederation provides our second example. The notion of the concurrent majority was advanced in the nineteenth century in the works and political activities of John C. Calhoun. No stranger to the intricacies of American government, the Sage of South Carolina served as a member of the House of Representatives, senator, secretary of war, secretary of state, and vice-president (under both John Q. Adams and Andrew Jackson). A staunch defender of states' rights and an advocate of the life-style of the agrarian south over that of the rapidly industrializing north, Calhoun argued that democratic theory in the contractual tradition de-

[14]Charles Secondat Baron de Montesquieu, *The Spirit of the Laws,* trans. Thomas Nugent (New York: Hafner Press, 1949), 127.

manded that critical decisions could be made only with the consent of all the relevant interests that would be affected by the outcome. In effect, this meant that a mere numerical majority was not adequate to prevail on a given issue unless it also represented the majority opinion of all the groups recognized as having an interest in the issue. As Calhoun himself articulated the argument in his famous "A Disquisition on Government," the concurrent majority

> give[s] to each division or interest, through its appropriate organ, either a concurrent voice in making and executing the laws or a veto on their execution. It is only by such an organism that the assent of each can be made necessary to put the government in motion or the power made effectual to arrest its action when put in motion; and it is only by the one or the other than the different interests, orders, classes, or portions into which the community may be divided can be protected.[15]

On its face, the notion of concurrent majorities has considerable appeal. It guarantees, for instance, that policies will not be undertaken unless or until they enjoy widespread support throughout the population. It also gives potentially exploitable minorities a powerful weapon with which to protect themselves against potentially tyrannical majorities. In practice, however, Calhoun's philosophy was used to justify nullification and secession, and to legitimate the continuation of slavery in the South and its extension into at least some of the new territories. Its usage in such fashions provides us with critical insights into its shortcomings. Like confederation generally, the concurrent majority disperses power, making coordinated public action difficult and national leadership all but impossible. It is, furthermore, inherently conservative, giving any small majority in any of the constituent groups virtual veto power over the expressed preference of even an overwhelming national majority. It can frustrate and obstruct the

---

[15] John C. Calhoun, *A Disquisition on Government* (Indianapolis: Bobbs-Merrill Co., 1953), 20.

will of a national majority and, as history has tragically demonstrated, make the peaceful resolution of contentious issues all but impossible.

A recent attempt to rehabilitate Calhoun's intellectual tradition provides the third and final example of representation by qualified majorities. The concept of consociationalism was born in the 1960s and 1970s from insightful observations by a number of scholars, including Bingham Powell, Jurg Steiner, Gerhard Lembruch and—perhaps most notably—Arend Lijphart. At the heart of their observations was the fact that a number of countries whose populations were badly fractured along ethnic, linguistic, racial, or religious lines, nevertheless enjoyed relatively stable regimes because their political elites were able to cooperate with one another. In countries as diverse as Malaysia, Canada, Cyprus, Austria, the Netherlands, and Switzerland consociational arrangements were observed as working or having worked in certain historical situations to sustain democratic rule in badly fractured societies.

According to Lijphart, who quotes Calhoun's "Disquisition" extensively, the key to consociational arrangements is the presence of a grand coalition, composed of the leader of each of the major segments that constitute the society, each of whom is armed with a "mutual veto"—the authority to reject unilaterally any measure he sees as a threat to his constituency.[16] In consociational states, the most important issues will be addressed by this coalition of elites, regardless of the existence of other formal governmental institutions. According to its proponents, such consociational arrangements elevate contentious issues out of the mass political arena, where they are likely to provoke sectional animosity, to the level of the elites, where they are more likely to be addressed peacefully.

Despite the expectations and efforts of its advocates, however, consociationalism has not worked in a number of situa-

---

[16] Arend Lijphart, *Democracy in Plural Societies: A Comparative Exploration* (New Haven: Yale University Press, 1977), 25–31.

tions where it has been imposed (for example, Northern Ireland), and it has not provided a panacea for precarious Third World countries facing severe internal dissension. In fact, it would appear that the success of consociationalism depends largely on a number of historically contingent factors (multiple societal segments, small national size, the geographical isolation or separation of the different societal segments, some basis for overarching national loyalty, some tradition of elite cooperation, and uncontested loyalty within each segment to its elite leadership) that cannot be artificially fabricated and that radically limit the list of candidate states for this type of representation. In short, the society that could best support such a system may be that, governmentally, in least need of it.

The final species of formal representation we need consider is the presidential-congressional system used in the United States. As a federated republic, the United States vertically distributes power amongst local, state, and national governments, although since the Civil War there has been little question that sovereign authority resides on the national level. More importantly, our system disperses power within the national government, as well as between it and the other levels of government. In effect, the founders established various political institutions, representing different—yet overlapping—constituencies. The presidency, with its national electorate, was designed to represent the entire country and to serve as its living embodiment, especially in international and military affairs. Conversely, the House of Representatives, whose members hail from smaller geographical districts, was structured to represent the more parochial interests of local constituents. Its two-year election cycle and preeminent power over the national purse strings keep it uniquely close to the local interests of the masses. The other half of the legislature, the Senate, was devised as an arena of representation for the constituent states and as an intermediary of sorts between the legislature and the president. Originally elected by state legislatures, senators are now chosen directly by the citizens of each state, but still—in most cases, at least—represent larger, more diverse constituencies. They may be less occupied with local interests, constituency service, and reelection concerns, and more disposed, therefore, to devote themselves to issues of more national import.

The founders also empowered an independent federal court system, charged with representing the nation's legal and constitutional traditions. More insulated than are its sister branches from the vicissitudes of daily political turmoil, the judiciary has in the twentieth century also become the representative arena for many unpopular minorities that cannot find adequate voice or protection elsewhere. Finally, yet another representative institution, not included in the framers' original plan, has developed in the federal bureaucracy. The nation's three million civilian federal employees are responsible for designing many of the rules that govern our daily lives and for implementing the laws passed by the Congress. Presiding at regulatory hearings, members of the bureaucracy often act as surrogate public representatives. In addition, the many professions represented in the bureaucratic corps all have ethical and performance codes, with which their members must comply, that ensure a certain level of responsibility and public accountability.

As the American case has proven, a presidential system can be very stable over time, with each individual institution of government—jealous of its own powers and suspicious of those possessed by others—serving as a vigilant watchdog on its sister branches. As the insightful James Madison observed two hundred years ago, ambition can indeed counteract ambition.

On the down side, a presidential system has definite liabilities, as well. As we must continually remind ourselves, this type of government was created by dyed-in-the-wool, classical liberals. The rhetoric of Alexander Hamilton notwithstanding, the founders' goal was not the creation of an active, vibrant state, but a limited and severely circumscribed one. According to the framers' common world view, which had been molded by the classical works of Hobbes and Locke, and hardened by the history of their own experiences with the British monarchy, the state was a potentially voracious enemy of freedom. The safety of the individual in society required that very tight reins be used on the state and its powers constantly monitored and checked. This view was reinforced by the founders' religious and economic beliefs that stressed individual initiative and underscored the responsibility of individuals for their own spiritual and material well-being. As a result, the founders perceived no need for—and many reasons to fear—a state with the power to interfere significantly in the lives of its citizens.

Institutionally, this philosophy is reflected in the fragmentation of power found in the federal government. While some form of majority rule or public accountability is stressed in all the branches, the requirement that *each* branch acquiesce in *every* decision conceals in the system a very profound antimajoritarian bias. From the conception of an idea to its passage as a law and its implementation as a policy, majority sanctions are needed at each of the torturous steps: in various legislative committees and subcommittees, on the floors of both chambers of Congress, in the executive branch, from at least one level of the federal judiciary (if the law is ever challenged on statutory or constitutional grounds), and in the pertinent bureaucratic agency or agencies. At any step of the way, a negative vote by any of the myriad of political actors involved—regardless of the preferences of all the other actors— can force compromises, delays, or even effectively scuttle a proposal, at least temporarily. When Vladimir Holan said that "[f]rom the sketch to the work one travels on one's knees," he was not referring to the American political process, but the image is still appropriate. Despite the appearance of majoritarian control at every stage of the process, the necessity for what are, in effect, concurrent majorities in a number of quite

disparate institutions can often frustrate the will of the national, popular majority.

In practice, presidential systems can be rigid and unresponsive. Designed to curtail and hobble the harmful use of
governmental power, the restraints built into this type of representation can also paralyze its ability to act in helpful or de-
sired ways. Since institutional unanimity is required for most
significant governmental actions, but any single institutional
actor can unilaterally veto many initiatives it does not like, a
crippling inactivity is often the result. This is especially true
in issue areas such as redistributive policy or innovative technologies, where powerful and entrenched minority interests
stand to lose quite a bit if the interests of the majority of society are allowed to prevail. History has shown, moreover,
that such minority interests can usually find a political champion in one of the institutions of government that is more
than willing to utilize its veto power to torpedo or the threat
of its veto to force major concessions in the majority's proposal. This provides one explanation for the relative rarity of
truly redistributive periods in American political history and
the relative scarcity of governmental support for promising,
"cutting-edge" technologies.

Having completed this relatively bleak assessment of the
various forms of representation, including our own presidential system, I must conclude the point where I started: we
face a serious problem of representation. Earlier, I argued
American history is largely the story of the expansion and the
meaningfulness of political participation through numerous
"bills of rights." It is the story of increased democratization
and enlarged suffrage. While the fears of elitists regarding the
radical tendencies of the masses have gone unrealized because of the uniquely restrained nature of the American political culture, the interest of the majority of Americans has
certainly been piqued and its expectations of majority rule
aroused. Unfortunately, as I suggested in my discussion of
our presidential system, our structure of governmental in-

stitutions was not designed to accommodate well the majority preferences of such a growing national electorate. In fact, exactly the opposite argument could be made. Efforts were undertaken during the founding to protect against precisely this type of majoritarian control; our government was designed to make it extremely difficult for any majority to control simultaneously the many different institutions necessary to sanction its preferences. Indeed, many of the framers and subsequent observers of their handiwork have argued that there were not enough safeguards against majority control built into the system. Writing some forty years after the founding, Toqueville contended that "[m]y greatest complaint against democratic government as organized in the United States is not, as many Europeans would make out, its weakness, but rather its irresistible strength. What I find most repulsive in America is not the extreme freedom reigning there but the shortage of guarantees against [a] tyranny [of the majority]." [17]

Yet, the historical march of democracy, with its expansion of suffrage and other forms of political participation, has run into the essentially countermajoritarian world view of the founders and the effectively antimajoritarian system of political institutions they created. The irresistible force of majority rule has met the immovable object of a basically sound, stable constitutional regime. The expectations generated by the former simply cannot be adequately met by the limited capacities of the latter. The result is a growing stress on the political culture, which includes a sense of frustration, political alienation, and deep-seated skepticism about the fairness of the entire political order.

This confrontation provides us with a profound intellectual problem and significant political opportunities. Intellectually, as I have suggested, we have a responsibility to follow in the

[17] Alexis de Tocqueville, *Democracy in America*, trans. George Lawrence, ed. J. P. Mayer (Garden City, N.Y.: Anchor Books, 1969), 252.

founders' footsteps and think critically about the nature of our political order. We must find within ourselves the intelligence and the imagination to step away from the exigencies of everyday political life and consider our situation from a greater distance. How can we alter our system to facilitate greater political representation and better protect the rights of minorities? And how can we do so while maintaining the principle of majority rule and yet protecting the integrity of the constitutional order and the long-term interests of society? Part of the answer to these questions lies in the overview of the various types of representation I have given above. The skeptical tenor and negative cast of that discussion were intentional. While each of the types of representation I discussed has definite advantages, they also all have severe shortcomings. I stress that because it is all too easy when criticizing our system to yearn for what appears to be far greener grass on the other side of the fence. But, despite the Pollyannaish rhetoric of those who advocate such radical changes, the grass on the other side is often not much greener and may—if I may overextend the metaphor—conceal a considerable variety of weeds. What is more, a change in our basic style of representation—to PR or corporatism, for instance—whatever its long-term advantages or disadvantages, would be extremely difficult to negotiate through our constitutional system. Every institution that would stand to lose power or authority under a proposed new system would have a say in the adoption of that system. It pushes the boundaries of credulity to believe such institutions would peacefully acquiesce to their own diminution.

If we assume, then, that a radical alteration in our kind of representation is beyond the pale of intellectual desirability and political practicality, we are left with a more limited, yet still significant, range of more traditional constitutional rearrangements. As the pressure on our system mounts, the need for some alteration in our institutions to allow them more readily to accommodate greater public participation and expectations will increase. Several viable proposals to enhance the quality of our representation by making the government more accountable to the people and responsible for its actions have been aired recently and demand our critical attention and appraisal. In the final lecture, when we consider the political opportunities to which our current situation has led us, we will give them just that.

CHAPTER 4

PARTY MAJORITIES AND PARTY MINORITIES: A MODEST PROPOSAL FOR CONSTITUTIONAL REFORM

AS WE BEGIN, a brief summing up of where we are is in order. First, I have contended that the United States has long endured a sometimes uneasy tension between concomitant desires for majority rule and individual rights. This tension began with the drafting, in Philadelphia, in the summer of 1787, of the Constitution—that marvelous blueprint for institutions and the formal mechanisms of government. Designed by Enlightenment men who were inherently suspicious of both governmental power and, to a lesser extent, of the people, this is a Constitution that divides, separates, and checks political power. It is, in fact, fair to say that the Constitution is an antimajoritarian charter, since the founders went to extreme institutional lengths to ensure that no popular majority could easily or quickly control the new government. This new order was radically altered, however, with the ratification of the Bill of Rights in 1791. Hardly two years after the signing of the Constitution, Congress adopted a new statement of Americans' political aspirations, one that emphasized individual rights and implied a wider public participation in political debate. The adoption of these ten amendments by the states signaled the awkward and uneasy coexistence in American political history of an eighteenth-century antimajoritarian set of institutions alongside an increasingly modern, participatory notion of democracy. That tension has continued to this day.

Second, this tension between institutions and popular participation has been exacerbated by what I have called the numerous informal "bills of rights" that we have added onto the original Bill of Rights. As the original Bill of Rights sounded the initial call for greater popular rights and public participation, six subsequent episodes in the American political drama have served to make that aspiration a reality. The rise and toleration of an opposition party, the development of judicial review, the emancipation of the black slaves and their subsequent enfranchisement, the granting of suffrage to women, the development of economic rights during the New Deal, and the struggle for social rights during the Great Society buttressed the trend in American history toward the concomitant expansion of both individual rights and the demands for more participatory—potentially majoritarian—rule.

Third, I have suggested that this growth of individual rights hand in glove with expanded majority rule has been possible because James Madison made a fundamental intellectual error, fearing a tension between majority rule and individual rights. In *Federalist* Ten and Fifty-one, he argued that only an extended national sphere could create the great diversity and heterogeneity necessary to curb and soften the potentially disastrous power of majority factions, and only a government of separated, jealous, and balanced institutions could be considered safe from such a factious takeover. What Madison failed to take adequate account of, however, was the nature of the American political culture. Far from being radical or factionalized, Americans were and are—as the insightful Tocqueville noticed in the 1830s—a largely quiescent, mild, and tolerant people, more interested in economic enterprises than political rabble-rousing. While American majorities have sometimes moved to the left, as the Roosevelt Democrats did in the 1930s, and sometimes to the right, as Reagan's Republicans have in the 1980s, they have not tended toward the extremes in either direction. The result has been that, historically, the American culture has been able to manage the simultaneous expansion of individual rights and political suffrage without undo harm to either.

Fourth, unfortunately, it seems as though this historical pattern may not be able to hold. As individual rights and public participation have increased under our "bills of rights," the conflict between the two halves of our constitutional system has hardened. At first the tension was mainly a theoretical one, the limited need for governmental services and the similarly limited extent of suffrage making for few practical problems with the country's institutional arrangements. As we have significantly extended the franchise and expanded popular rights, however, while doing little to alter the basic institutional assumptions of the Constitution of 1787, problems have arisen. In particular, public expectations have been heightened, resulting in increasing demands upon the governmental structures. Our institutional arrangements, however, which were designed to protect society rather than accommodate particular groups and are in most important respects unchanged from the founding, are resistant to majority control and susceptible to systemic deadlock.

The fifth and final point I have emphasized is the somber thought that there is no single, simple, painless panacea for the political malady that afflicts us. Although there are a number of alternative kinds of democratic representation that are viable under certain conditions, they all have severe limitations and some rather unpleasant side effects. In addition, a change to any one of the alternative styles of representation would be extremely hard to accomplish politically. The political actors who would have to sanction any such reform are, we must remember, winners under the present system and hence would be reluctant to change the rules of a game they have learned to play so well. We must realize, quite simply, that unlike the founders we will not have the luxury of creating a national political system basically de novo. Our institutions are well-entrenched and most identifiable interests well-organized and mobilized. All of these factors place significant limits on the kinds and extent of reforms our political system can peacefully process.

I would now like to return to the challenge I set at the beginning of this discussion when I said that one of my few disappointments in this bicentennial year has been the lack of critical attention focused on the current state of our constitutional order. This dearth of cerebration offers a dire contrast to the founders' profound ability to examine, critique, and improve upon their existing political regime (that is, the Articles of Confederation) that led them to write, adopt, and ratify the Constitution that we are celebrating. The framers were able, in a manner almost unique in the history of western man, to rise above the purely temporal considerations of the times and plan a constitutional arrangement they felt would be fair, safe, flexible, and republican. They did their best—and an excellent job it was—to build institutions that correlated well with the political values they held very dearly. In short, they accomplished a difficult intellectual task. They abstracted themselves and achieved the critical distance necessary to view their world with discrimination—and with imagination. They then planned how they could change it for the better, and—matching intellectual rigor with political skill—they followed through on their insights in order to accomplish the founding.

Since time has not stood still since 1787, since many of our values have changed—or at least broadened—in the past two centuries, and since the world we live in has mutated into a very different place from that known to the framers, we are now called to a similar task. Like our founding fathers, we, too, are faced with an existing political order in need of an overhaul, and we, too, must be constitution makers. We must strive to find within ourselves the critical, insightful attitude about politics that motivated their work in the summer of 1787. In sum, we must struggle to rise above mere self-interest and political exigency, to think in more rarefied terms of arrangements that could ease our political tensions, to re-form our institutions to reflect more accurately our modern values, and to remain fair and forward-looking as a people and in our polity. As we conclude, I will, as promised, outline some of my recommendations for how this reformed constitutional order—one that better ensures both majority rule and individual rights—should be arranged.

What I am going to suggest is not, however, a new idea. In fact, what I advocate more than anything else is a return to a kind of party government similar to what we had in this country one hundred years ago. Before discussing how our party government of the nineteenth century developed, operated, and then went into decline, I should note its theoretical dimensions. Reversing the usual terms "majority party" and "minority party," I call the kind of partisan governance I envision "party majority and party minority representation." Constitutionally, this entails a system that is hospitable toward—even demanding of—government by a party majority, with strong opposition from a party minority. The operative word in these terms is *party*. The point requires emphasis because I see a sharp distinction between "party" and "public," between a party majority and a plebiscitary majority. Whether it is found in a town meeting, in a referendum, in an initiative, or in a mob, a plebiscitary majority tends to be an extremely ephemeral, thin, shifting phenomenon. It is often poorly anchored in the constituency, more likely supported by people responding to a temporary emotional surge rather than to any reasoned evaluation of their long-term interests. Plebiscitary majorities are sometimes irrational and ever irresponsible, caring less for the long-term health of the political system than for their members' diverse and parochial interests.

Party majorities, on the other hand, are a different breed. They tend to be more continuous groups, possessed of more consistent attitudes. Party majorities are organized, ongoing, and institutionalized. They have a recognizable leadership cadre, followers who are rather strongly committed to the party on both affective and policy grounds, an institutional memory, and—as ongoing actors in the political drama—a commitment to the long-term health of the polity. What is perhaps most important, because parties are continuous, is that they can be held responsible for their actions. While a plebiscitary majority evaporates after voting, a party does not. It takes a stand, implements a policy, and then, based on the consequences of the policy, may be held accountable by the public. In a word, party majorities tend to be disciplined.

This process is enhanced if there is also a party minority, which, acting as the public's surrogate memory, is ever vigilant to remind the people exactly whom they should hold responsible for failed policy initiatives. Proof that a party majority/party minority system can operate well and that the people are willing to hold a party responsible for its failings can be found in the New Deal experience. For over a decade after the unlucky Herbert Hoover, who really had done his best to alleviate the suffering brought on by the Great Depression, was defeated by Franklin Roosevelt, in 1932, the Democrats ran not so much against their Republican opposition as they did against the memory of Hoover, whom they portrayed as a cold, flinty, uncaring man. In every election, presidential and congressional, between 1934 and 1944, the Democratic Party flayed the memory of Hoover's ineffectual economic policies and held the specter of failed Republican policies up for public inspection. While this may seem somewhat unkind and unfair, it is an effective means of ensuring that parties realize they will be held accountable—for years to come—for the choices they make and, hence, should make such decisions with extreme care. Today, decades after Lyndon Johnson and Jimmy Carter left office, the Democratic Party still suffers from popular memories of their failures and shortcomings.

As accustomed as we are to the presence of political

parties—however weak and ineffective they may seem in the present epoch—we must remember that the founders not only made no provisions for the emergence of parties, but were keenly opposed to the very notion of party governance.

While historians disagree about the exact origins of such institutions, nascent political organizations had emerged in England at least by the restoration of Charles II (1660–1685), when parliamentary factions began to coalesce into what would later become the Whig and Tory parties. By the time of the American Revolution, the English parties were recognizable as such, with the Tories having become the party of the "court" and the Whigs the party of the "country."

Since Americans lay much of the blame for the Revolution on the fractious Parliament, the prevalent postwar attitude in the former colonies was one singularly suspicious of political parties. In the famed Essex Result of 1778, Theophilus Parsons warned of the dangers of parties in legislative settings. If parties were allowed to form in popular assemblies, he cautioned, "[t]he members would list under the banners of their respective leaders: address and intrigue would conduct the debates, and the result would tend only to promote the ambitions or interest of a particular part."[1] Speaking more generally, both Hamilton and Madison in *The Federalist*, advised against their use. In the very first paper published by "Publius," Hamilton cautioned of the "intolerant spirit which has at all times characterized political parties."[2] Later in *Federalist* 50, Madison characterized parties as engendering violent hatred and rage.

The new nation's political leaders held out the hope that, beginning virtually from scratch, they could create a pure political order that would operate only in the public interest, without the factious interference of organized, self-interested

[1] Quoted in Charles S. Hyneman and Donald S. Lutz, eds., *American Political Writing During the Founding Era* (Indianapolis: Liberty Press, 1983), 1:498.

[2] Hamilton, Jay, and Madison, *The Federalist* (see chap. 1, n. 6), 5.

political parties. In fact, there was much concern during George Washington's presidency about the very legitimacy of any sort of organized political opposition. As William Nesbitt Chambers has observed, "Washington was convinced that once the new national government had been put in his hands, it was up to him and his chosen aides to manage it."[3] The first president went so far in attempting to prevent the growth of an opposition party as to invite both the Republican Jefferson and the Federalist Hamilton to serve as his principal advisers. As late as 1797, when he was clearly able to see the nascent Republican-Federalist split, Washington still clung to the hope that partisan rivalries could be avoided and counseled against their growth. "[T]he baneful effects of the spirit of party," Washington stated unforgettably in his farewell address,

> serves always to distract the public councils and enfeeble the public administration. It agitates the community with ill-founded jealousies and false alarms; kindles the animosity of one part against another; foments occasionally riot and insur-rection. It opens the door to foreign influence and corruption.[4]

As we know, Washington's advice was not to prevail. The severe sectional, economic, and policy differences between the Hamiltonian Federalists and the Jeffersonian Republicans overwhelmed Washington's best efforts and resulted in the birth of the two-party system during the late 1790s and the election of 1800. Although they were nowhere mentioned in the Constitution of 1787, the new political parties quickly be-came the focal points of electoral activity. For several reasons, however, neither of the new parties developed the kind of po-litical character or exercised the level of political control that parties later in the century would. One reason for this is that the Federalist Party, the party of Washington, Adams, and

---

[3] William Nesbitt Chambers, *Political Parties in a New Nation: The American Experience, 1776–1809* (New York: Oxford University Press, 1965), 5.
[4] Commager, *Documents of American History* (see chap. 2, n. 1), 172.

Hamilton, was overwhelmed by the Jeffersonian realignment during the early years of the nineteenth century. As the suffrage spread to new voters along the frontier who had been alienated by the Federalists' commercial policies, the electoral fortunes of the elitist Federalists plummeted. By the end of Jefferson's second term, the party had ceased to function nationally for all practical purposes, and the country entered a period of one-party (really no-party) control, euphemistically called the "era of good feeling."

A more important reason for the limited extent of the first parties in the United States was the limited nature of the government of the times. Parties are, by design, political instruments used to link the governed with the governors. As long as the governors were not engaging in much activity, there was little interest among the governed and little need for well-developed linkage mechanisms. A look at the federal budgets for the period tells much of the story. Between 1800 and the start of the War of 1812, federal expenditures for the entire nation never rose above eleven million dollars a year. The lion's share of each year's budget was split between the War Department and payments on the nation's public debt. The government did little else. There were few internal improvement programs, only a small bureaucracy, little pork to fill the barrel, and few government contracts. What little the government was doing was happening in the nation's new, largely inaccessible, terribly dull capital on the Potomac River.

In the District of Columbia, what parties there were during the nation's first forty years of existence were what James Sterling Young has termed "boardinghouse cliques."[5] In the rented rooms of the nation's capital, legislators associated on a sectional basis, living and taking their meals with other congressmen and senators from their region. Lacking much contact with their constituents, legislators found that their sec-

---

[5]James Sterling Young, *The Washington Community, 1800–1828* (New York: Harcourt Brace Jovanovich, 1966), 98–106.

tional colleagues provided an excellent political reality check, since, coming from similar districts, they were aware of the people's concerns. Still, for all practical purposes, these party affiliations existed only in Washington—what today we would call "inside the beltway"—and did not serve to link the government with the people. Because of the limited scope of government and the subsequent lack of popular interest in it, the institutional arrangements initiated by the founders were adequate to the task. While the founders had not succeeded in preventing the emergence of parties, they had created a governmental structure capable of functioning with only rudimentary, poorly organized party groupings.

This constitutional order, in which official governmental institutions were supreme, was soon to end. As the suffrage was extended to more and more ordinary citizens, and as doctrines such as Henry Clay's "American system" began to rationalize a more active federal role in society, more powerful political parties developed. Parties began to be seen as mechanisms for translating popular preferences into government policy. A regime that had been designed to limit the power of government by breaking the power of parties and inhibiting their growth found itself transforming under popular pressure into a constitutional order in which political parties would perform key functions in terms of organizing the government and linking it with the voting population.

The party majority and party minority system that emerged during the 1830s and reached its acme during the Republican Party dominance of the period from 1860–1910 provided the nation with the partisan leadership necessary to settle the sectional "nature of the union" dispute and to lead it during a period of unparalleled economic growth. At the beginning of the Republican Party, the issue of the union was becoming paramount, and the party's organizers could not have foreseen that it would one day become the "party of business." Indeed, at its inception, the one ideological item that tied its disparate elements together was an opposition to the spread of slavery into the new territories. The Civil War was not generally favored by Northern businesses, which at the start of hostilities lost one of their largest markets and had to write off many large debts held by Southerners. Contrary to the expectations of Northern capital, however, the war turned out to be a boon to industrial interests. There were lucrative government contracts to be had, tariffs were raised, currency was nationalized, government loans were made available to war-related enterprises, and public land grants were handed out to the railroads and real estate developers—all of which served to make Northern industrialists quite happy with the Grand Old Party.

After the war, Republican support of industrialization continued. Unlike the Democracy, which identified itself with the agrarian legacy of Jefferson and Jackson, the Republican Party had little ideological baggage to inhibit its wholehearted support of capitalism. In the period from 1870 at least until the New Deal, the GOP was the political arm of the members of the ascendant new business class; it was controlled by them, represented their interests, and provided the political transmission belt by which they controlled the government. The key political issues during the last part of the nineteenth century were economic ones: sound money programs, high tariffs, aid to railways, national banks, labor unrest. The Republican Party sided with industry on all these issues and enjoyed an almost uninterrupted period of political supremacy.

Although many historians ignore this period as boring, I think it interesting from the point of view of representation. The leadership of the Republican Party represented the emerging business elite and the cause of economic development. Although we may not like all the results of this development—and I will address those in a moment—it was just this kind of development that the country needed at that time. Under largely Republican tutelage, the nation evolved from an agricultural state and a marginal world power into a vibrant industrial polity at the center of the world economic stage. Between 1870 and 1928, the United States grew from a country in which over half the population still worked on the farm into the world's largest industrial state with over one-third of the globe's manufacturing capacity. During this period the per capita national product tripled and the scope of production greatly enlarged as cottage industries gave way to assembly lines with their tremendous economies of scale.

Politically, the Grand Old Party dominated the landscape. During the seventy-two years from Abraham Lincoln's election in 1860 until Franklin D. Roosevelt rewrote the political record books in 1932, only two Democrats—Grover Cleveland and Woodrow Wilson—occupied the White House. Moreover, of these two, Cleveland was a "gold" Democrat and highly sympathetic to business concerns, and Wilson won in 1912 only because of a serious split in the Republican Party. In the Congress, the Republican dominance was almost as marked. Of the thirty-five Congresses from the start of the Civil War until the end of Hoover's presidency (the Thirty-seventh through the Seventy-second Congresses), Democrats held electoral majorities in the House only eleven times and controlled the Senate a mere five times.

The period is remembered among congressional historians as the apogee of party control under powerful Republican committee chairmen and forceful speakers. Men like Thomas Brackett Reed and Joseph Cannon held the House in an iron grip, and hence were effective in implementing the policy preferences of the majority party over the obstructionist tactics of the minority. Finally, still located in a small chamber in the center of the Capitol between the two houses of Congress, the Supreme Court—its conservative members appointed by the long string of Republican presidents—stood as a bulwark against any laws, federal or state, that made it past the numerous legislative hurdles. In cases such as *Lochner v. New York, Adair v. United States, Hammer v. Dagenhart,* and others, the high court struck down efforts to limit the freedoms of businessmen in matters such as setting the length of a workday, requiring union nonmembership as a condition of employment, and using child labor, thus setting itself firmly in the camp of the industrialists.

In short, the Republican Party of the latter-nineteenth and early-twentieth centuries was the majority party of its day and acted like it. It was effective in organizing the ascendant business classes, translating their support into votes, and those votes into government policy. By providing a common ideology and tying together the various branches of government behind a common agenda, the Republican Party overcame the fractionalizing tendencies of the checks-and-balances system. The GOP of that time was representative of the more vibrant element of society, capable of building an electoral majority and willing to be held accountable by that majority for its success or failure. Of equal importance, despite the shrill protestations of many Democrats at the time, the Republicans were able to accomplish what they did without undo violence to the political rights of other groups in society. In an era of expanding suffrage, the Republicans simply could not afford to alienate large segments of the population for fear these groups would mobilize or be mobilized by the Democrats against them.

This stable period of party majority/party minority government sowed the seeds of its own demise during the early part of the twentieth century, as it came under increasing assault from several fronts. The first of these was the industrial-reform movement. Although the economic growth engineered under Republican Party leadership had tremendous aggregate benefits for the nation as a whole, the industrial thrust left vast human wreckage in its wake. Manufacturing wages, despite the huge leap in output, had risen to an average of only a dollar and a half a day by 1890—women and children who worked in the factories made far less. Working conditions were unregulated and extremely hazardous; long working days, often in excess of twelve hours, were common. The workers' living conditions, often in ramshackle, crowded, filthy, company-owned tenements, were primitive. While a few lucky entrepreneurs lived their own private Horatio Alger stories, the lives of most industrial workers were grinding, unhealthy, and dangerous.

Not just industrial workers, but the average consumer as well, paid a high price for the nation's economic "progress." In the rush to make profits, many manufacturers cut dangerous corners and produced harmful, impure, or badly flawed products; in the frenzied, unregulated competition of the day, many engaged in business practices ignoring or ignorant of the social consequences that would follow. Perhaps the best summary of growing attitudes toward the human cost of the nation's economic thrust is to be found in the literature of the period. Works like Upton Sinclair's *The Jungle*, describing the unsanitary practices of the Chicago stockyards, and Frank Norris's *The Octopus*, cataloging the unscrupulousness of the wheat and railroad industries, dramatized the flesh-and-blood, human costs of the period. Growing popular revulsion with the industrial excesses of the period was directed not only against the manufacturers themselves but also at the party with which they were associated. It is not surprising, then, that when the industrial reforms of the twentieth century undermined the economic power of the industrial class, the Republican Party's bastion of strength, public confidence in the party and in the philosophy of social Darwinism it espoused, was shaken as well.

To a certain extent, the blame for the demise of the strong parties can also be laid at the feet of the Republican Party's congressional leadership. During the early part of this century, ideological rifts began to develop between the reform-minded Republicans in the executive branch and the GOP's "Old Guard" in the Congress, which became increasingly autocratic and capricious. Speaker Joseph Cannon symbolized the problem. A longtime representative from Illinois, Cannon became speaker in 1903 and ruled over the House until he was "overthrown" in 1910–1911. Through his control of the

Rules Committee and the committee appointment power, he exercised pervasive influence over the chamber, able to make or break careers by virtue of whom he assigned to what committees. Uncompromising toward his enemies, Cannon represented the conservative faction of his party, which was opposed to many of the era's social, economic, and political reform movements. Some of the speaker's obdurateness and limited social vision is summed up in his famous response to Teddy Roosevelt's recommendations for environmental legislation: "Not one cent for scenery."[6]

As we know, Cannon's ruthless, czarlike ways and reactionary policy positions made him many enemies in government and in the House itself. By holding the reins of power so tightly, the speaker alienated many of his fellow partisans—especially high-ranking committee chairs—who felt they should be given more say in the formulation of legislation. The pressure broke in 1910, when the House, behind insurgent Republican committee chairmen, voted to strip the speaker of his appointment power and remove him from the Rules Committee. That move effectively enfeebled the congressional party leadership and began a process of power decentralization that has continued to the present day.

The other internal feature that contributed to the breakup of the strong party system was the corruption that had eaten into both major parties by the early years of this century. In the nation's major cities "partisan machines" were founded to help lubricate the cogs of the political process. Money often changed hands, favors were traded, votes were bought and sold, nepotism was rampant, elections were rigged, mail fraud was not unheard of, and connections with illegal businesses (gambling, prostitution, bootlegging) were widespread. Most urban businesses—licit or illicit—quickly learned that, if they hoped to prosper, they should cooperate

[6]Quoted in William Henry Harbaugh, *Power and Responsibility: The Life and Times of Theodore Roosevelt* (New York: Farrar, Straus and Cudahy, 1961), 321.

with the local party machine. Reformers of the period, who felt that government could and should be conducted on a more ethical basis, found in the partisan machines a suitable target for their wrath. Representing, as they did, cronyism, graft, and corruption of all kinds, the machines came under increasing pressure from well-organized reform movements during the twentieth century. An unfortunate side effect of their gradual dismantling was that the parties, one of the few integrative forces in American politics—whatever their many shortcomings—were seared in the fire storm of the municipal reform movement.

A battery of reforms reduced the party bastions. In the cities, reformers pushed for a depoliticization of municipal functions. Starting in 1913, many cities began to adopt council-manager systems. Such arrangements included a small city council, whose five to seven members were elected at large from the city as a whole, and a professionally trained city manager, who handled the day-to-day operations of the city and answered to the council. The at-large elections for council members were seen as limiting the power of ward bosses, and the professional city managers as less subject to political corruption. Serving only as figureheads, mayors under council-manager arrangements were stripped of much of the patronage power and political pork they had at their disposal under other forms of municipal governments. Because of its ability to break the power of many corrupt municipal partisan machines, the council-manager became and remains the preferred choice of most municipal reformers.

Another critical political reform during this era was the switch from the partisan to the so-called Australian ballot. Before the 1870s most ballots used in political elections were printed by the parties themselves and distributed to their members as they came to the polls to vote. The partisan ballots were, in effect, straight-ticket ballots, listing only the names of the party's candidates. If you were a registered Democrat and went to the polls, you were given a Democratic ballot, which was conspicuously colored to distinguish it from the Republican ballot. You then cast this ballot publicly so that everyone—particularly the local party leadership—knew for whom you voted. Beginning in the 1880s, however, reformers began to replace the party ballots with a new ballot form borrowed from Australia. These new "Australian rules" ballots were printed at public expense; listed both parties' candidates for each office on a single, uniform sheet; allowed each voter to choose between the candidates listed; and were cast in secret. By the beginning of the twentieth century the Australian ballots were in use in virtually every public election in the nation. The ostensible reason for the introduction of the new ballots was to reduce voting corruption. Since the ballots were marked and cast in secret, potential vote buyers could never be certain that the vote they paid for would actually be delivered.

An unforeseen consequence of the Australian ballot was the increased ticket splitting that followed in its wake. Since the new ballot allowed voters to pick and choose amongst the candidates offered by the two parties, many did so. Instead of voting for all the Democrats on the ticket, as they would have done if given party ballots, Democratic voters looking, in secret, at Australian ballots could easily select their own party's candidate for the Congress, but the Republican nominee for the presidency. Indeed, Jerrold Rusk and others have found empirical evidence of a significant increase in split-ticket voting after the adoption of the Australian ballot.[7] The result of this decline in party discipline in the voting booth has been, of course, an increased fractionalization of government. As ticket splitting increases, so do the chances that the basic institutions of government—on the national, state, and local levels—will not all be under the control of the same party. Given the vast arsenal of institutional checks and bal-

[7]See Jerrold Rusk, "The Effect of the Australian Ballot Reform on Split Ticket Voting," *American Political Science Review* (December 1970), 1220–38.

ances in our constitutional order, splitting control of the major institutions between the two parties cannot but contribute to systemic paralysis. Whatever the Australian ballot's virtues in terms of reducing electoral corruption, its splintering impact on control of governmental institutions must be acknowledged and addressed.

Another political reform of the progressive era that had a profound negative impact on the strong party system was the institution of a competitive, professional civil-service system. Before the 1880s most civilian employees of the federal government were appointed by the president (on the basis of partisan recommendation) as a reward for their political support. The so-called spoils system, associated with Andrew Jackson, who greatly expanded its use, was the principal means by which the presidential administrations of the nineteenth century staffed the executive branch. Eventually, the excesses of this system began to cause severe problems. Incompetent appointees were commonplace and undermined public confidence in government. With every change in administrations, virtually the entire executive payroll was replaced with new appointees, contributing to a sense of near constant turmoil in Washington, which was not helped by increasingly intense political battles between the Congress and the executive over controversial appointees. Finally, requests for patronage appointments became, as the federal government grew in size and responsibility, increasingly burdensome on the presidents, who were deluged with requests for positions. The impact of this situation was tragically driven home in 1881 when, a few months after his inauguration, President James A. Garfield was assassinated by Charles J. Guiteau, a frustrated office seeker.

Largely because of the perceived evils of the patronage system, steps were taken in 1883 to professionalize the civil service. The Civil Service Reform Act, which is better known as the Pendleton Act, attempted to reform the federal bureaucracy along the lines suggested by the professional British civil service. It established a merit system—complete with competitive examinations—for federal appointments, demanded partisan neutrality of bureaucrats during their tenure of public service, and, in exchange, offered civil servants a great deal of employment protection once they were in office. The Pendleton Act also established the United States Civil Service Commission to oversee the federal bureaucracy. Although originally intended to cover only some 15 percent of federal employees, the civil-service system has been gradually extended so that today it includes virtually all executive-branch employees, excepting only a few thousand high-level political appointees.

As the professional civil service expanded in the federal government and came to be used as a model for state and local government employment practices as well, another pillar of party government was eroded. No longer could the parties use their appointment powers as the great political pork barrel they had been in the past. Education, specialized skills, and examination scores came to replace party loyalty as the key requirements necessary to land a government job. As the professional bureaucratic ethos spread throughout government, moreover, the delivery of governmental goods and services was also radically altered. In effect, the provision of governmental services was depoliticized and the political parties removed as the intermediaries between the political producers and the political consumers. If a citizen needed a governmental contract or a pension or his street repaired, he no longer took his request to the local political party, but to a nonpartisan bureaucratic agency, whose explicit purpose was to be as equitable, uniform, and unbiased as possible. Again, regardless of the undoubted benefits of governmental professionalization and bureaucratization (for example, less corruption, more efficient service), these reforms also reduced the benefits parties could distribute among their members and, hence, contributed to their demise as potent political forces.

A final political reform that we must note involved a radical change in the manner in which political candidates were chosen. Prior to the reform era, most parties chose their political champions in relatively closed, convention systems. Small affairs, involving few people, these conventions could easily be controlled by the parties' elite leadership cadres, whose powers make those of today's "superdelegates" seem puny indeed. The conventions, in effect, gave the most committed, informed, and active elements within each party the power to choose the party's nominees for the offices being contested. The result was, usually, the selection of experienced, loyal, well-known candidates to carry the party's banner into the election. Candidates selected through a party's convention process knew to whom they owed their fealty, tended to be ideologically compatible, and were usually well known to the other candidates. Consequently, if they were eventually elected, there was a cohesiveness to the party's office holders. They believed in a common party platform, were well enough acquainted to work well together, and knew their partisan endorsement could be retracted if they failed to hold to the publicly advertised party line.

Suspicious of the tight control parties exercised over the electoral process, many reformers in the latter 1800s pushed for more direct "popular" input into the selection of partisan nominees. Although primaries had been used in numerous local elections since at least the early 1840s, they did not become popular at the state level until the La Follette Progressives latched onto the idea late in the century. After an intensive, decade-long battle, Wisconsin adopted a statewide primary in 1903, the first state to do so. Others soon followed suit, so that by 1915 some kind of primary was in use throughout the union. Instituted to make the electoral process more democratic, primaries effectively hobbled partisan government. With the candidate selection process thrown open to a popular vote of "partisan identifiers" and "independents," the party leadership was robbed of its most crucial function. No longer could the active, informed, committed core of the party effectively exercise a quality control on its own candidates. Indeed, the new primary system invited aspiring candidates to appeal over the heads of the leadership directly to the public, and that is precisely what they did. To use a football analogy, the primary reforms stripped the parties' coaching staffs of their ability to call plays and choose players, and made all those decisions contingent upon a vote of spectators in the stands. In politics, as on the gridiron, that is not a prescription for a very competitive strategy or productive contest.

In addition to these political reforms, two other developments have weakened parties in this century: the rise of the imperial presidency and of our ubiquitous media. During the period of strong party control, the party's national leaders were important and powerful people. They were capable of making or undoing a political career; even presidents took care not to cross the leadership cadre. A party's national leadership was the institutional party made manifest; it represented the party's philosophy, programs, and unity. Perhaps no one characterized this kind of partisan leader more than Marcus A. Hanna. An Ohio banking and industrial magnate, "Dollar Mark" led the Republican Party during the 1890s and early 1900s. He was influential in guiding the career of his political protégé William McKinley, chaired the national committee in 1896, and served in the Senate from 1897 until his death in 1904. Although he is largely forgotten today, except by historians, during the nation's period of Republican dominance, Hanna—and others almost as powerful—exercised wide influence over political affairs in Congress and at the White House.

In the modern era, party leaders enjoy no such authority. Today, when their party is out of power, national party chairpersons are merely one voice among the many clamoring to speak for the party. When their party is in power, they have even less prestige, becoming virtually staff assistants to the president. In fact, they are not even senior advisers, being at the beck and call of even junior White House assistants. I remember a Democratic party chairman once confiding to me that he "could not even go to the john in the morning" without clearing it first with someone in the executive office. We have invested tremendous authority in the presidency, while decreasing the office's reliance on political parties. The president is responsible for a huge bureaucracy, a trillion-dollar budget, the military security of the west, the nation's economy—in sum, the day-to-day operations of the largest, wealthiest, mightiest democracy in the world—and virtually none of this is contingent upon support from his party.

Ever since Teddy Roosevelt—"that damned cowboy," as Mark Hanna called him[8]—discovered that the presidency was a "bully pulpit" and that he could run a competitive campaign without the support of the Republican establishment, the link between the chief executive and his party has been tenuous at best. Presidential candidates are no longer screened and tapped by the party's leadership to carry the banner; rather, they put together their own primary campaigns with little help from the leadership. Once nominated, candidates maintain a certain distance from the party—often virtually running against it, as Jimmy Carter did in 1976. They build their own temporal coalitions, choose their own issues (feeling free to ignore party platform planks they disagree with), and pick their own staffs. Moreover, nominees receive but little support from the party. In 1980, Jimmy Carter and Ronald Reagan together spent some thirty-four million dollars in their contest for the presidency. Of this total, less than four million—approximately 12 percent—came from their respective parties. While we think little of this today, having become inured to the incapacity of our parties and the independence of our presidents, in many other polities the idea that the

[8] Hanna also once referred to Roosevelt as a "madman." See Henry F. Pringle, *Theodore Roosevelt: A Biography* (New York: Harcourt, Brace and Co., 1931), 223, and H. H. Kohlsaat, *From McKinley to Harding* (New York: Scribner's, 1923), 101.

party leadership should be so completely subordinate to or ignored by the elected executive leadership would be quite strange. I contend that we *should* consider it odd—and unacceptable—as well.

Finally, there are the media. While the media provide a wonderfully handy—and often improbable—scapegoat for every societal ill from drug abuse to reckless driving, their ascendance in the twentieth century has had a negative impact on political parties. Before the development of the modern, all-pervasive media, political events were mediated for the people by the parties. In the precincts and districts and wards, the parties performed a critical intermediary role. Politicians, incapable of reaching the people directly, had to take their messages to the masses largely through the party machinery. Likewise, if people had an issue they wanted placed on the political agenda, there were no television networks or popular news magazines to whom they could appeal. Rather, they had to make their case to the partisan leadership. That no longer obtains.

Today, a president or any other politician with a problem does not take it to the party or even to copartisans in other elective offices. Instead, the first instinct is to appeal over the heads of the party directly to the people. Politicians no longer need a partisan filter; they are capable of campaigning directly with the people. As a result, the new political kingpins are the media personalities and the media consultants whom politicians hire to present their images to the TV-watching public. This in itself is not so bad; what is pernicious is the tendency of the media toward extreme superficiality. Playing to a public audience that is often not terribly well versed in politics or even very interested in it, the media strive to make their coverage "relevant"—read "exciting." Stories on the nightly network news are designed to be short and flashy; they can do no more than hit the highlights of any given issue, and since TV is a visual medium, stories are sometimes not carried at all if they do not include good film footage.

To keep the public's interest, media reportage often focuses on personalities rather than issues, images at the expense of substance, and crisis rather than continuity. The result is a trivialization of politics and a distorted public perception of the political process. Issues, which are often resistant to coverage in a thirty-second "spot," are largely ignored, while the reporters—and, therefore, the public—focus on President Johnson's appendectomy scar, Senator Simon's bow tie, and the ever-present narrowing or widening popularity polls. Moreover, since some institutions, like the presidency, are more amenable to television coverage than are others (for example, the Congress, which with its 535 members looks chaotic, or the Supreme Court, which operates with judicious secrecy), public perception of the executive branch is artificially enhanced at the expense of others. In addition, since the media focus on the exciting and unusual, rather than the mundane and ordinary—regardless of which is more important—the popular perception of government is skewed, with people often believing the government of the day is far more unstable, incompetent, unprepared, scandal-ridden and crises-beset than it is. In the absence of much partisan loyalty to serve as a political anchor, such perceptions contribute to wide swings and lunges in public preference.

Now, looking back at these reform movements, we can grant that they were well intentioned and that following the reforms, Americans have enjoyed more honest, less corrupt, and more evenhanded government than before. But these advantages have not been purchased without a very high price, paid in the currency of effective partisan governance. In essence, whatever the ancillary benefits accrued from their demise, a political void has been left where the parties used to be. The partisan glue that held the political system together has largely melted away. As the parties have shrunk, many of the incentives that the president had to cooperate with the Congress, or the House to cooperate with the Senate, have disappeared. No longer do we have strong party majorities and party minorities capable of fighting out ideological and political battles over the course of decades. Instead, we have a collection of mostly self-interested office holders, with at best a minimal commitment to their parties, who seek in elections to put *their* electoral coalitions together for their individual advancement.

The kind of government we have in this postreform period is a Madisonian one. Governmental power has been distributed (every politician has the capacity to appeal directly to the people), separated (with the rise of split-ticket voting, the electoral linkage between the president and the Congress has been all but severed), and checked (political coalitions are ephemeral and fickle; without the acquiescence of all parties, little can be done). Yes, Madison realized his goal—a system in which ambition has been made to counteract ambition, and individual electoral aspirations have been made to counteract collective electoral aspirations. The Constitution of 1787, the institutional constitution, which sought deliberately to divide government in the interests of liberty, has prevailed.

All this is not a matter of merely "academic" concern. From my perspective, the principal result has been a deterioration in the quality of governance and the development of a pattern of government that oscillates between stalemate and spasm. Absent the integrative forces of partisan unity, the various institutions of government often deadlock over issues. As a result, they are largely unable to anticipate problems, plan ahead, or make provisions for gradual, controlled change. In the face of an impending crisis, there is a long period of delay, institutional stalemate, and political impotence. Then, when the crisis breaks, there is a spasm, a sudden, belated burst of activity during which actions that should have been taken carefully years before are done hurriedly, expensively, poorly, and—because crises fade—incompletely.

This is a systemic problem, as exemplified by midterm elections. As one of the many means of fragmenting power, the Constitution, of course, provides different timetables for the elections to different offices. Senators are elected to six-year terms, presidents to a four-year tenure, and members of the House of Representatives must run for reelection every other year. While there may be many good reasons for this complex schedule of elections—and it is defended most eloquently in *The Federalist*—one of its untoward consequences is that half-way through a president's term of office the entire House and one-third of the Senate stand for reelection. In the twentieth century these midterm elections have—with one exception, 1934—shared a common characteristic: the president's party has lost seats in the House of Representatives. Sometimes the loss is as small as five seats, other times as large as forty-eight; the postwar average has been thirty-one. The upshot is that right in the middle of a president's term, after he has struggled to build a working relationship with the Congress and as he strives to push his legislative agenda through to fruition, the political battle lines are redrawn, with the president's forces holding a strategically poorer position. This is always frustrating for a president and—as I will demonstrate—sometimes fateful for the nation. While political scientists disagree about what causes midterm slumps, their consequences are clear. Lacking the national drama that presidential-election years hold, congressional battles in the midterm are fought on local turfs over local issues. Unfortunately, they have national consequences in that they alter the balance of power in the Congress and are interpreted by the party out of power as a mandate to repudiate the president's policies. This fuels the alternation of deadlock and spasm that I have discussed and contributes to the frustrating tendency of our system to sputter to a standstill halfway into a policy initiative.

A couple of examples may make the point more clearly. The first concerns President Woodrow Wilson and his fight for the League of Nations. In the fall of 1918, as World War I ended with an abrupt armistice and the Versailles peace conference was set to convene, America was voting to elect the members of the Sixty-sixth Congress. Aware of the fact that his contro-

versial "Fourteen Point" proposal for lasting peace would require eventual Senate approval in its treaty form, Wilson campaigned for Democratic congressional candidates that fall,
urging the American people to return a Democratic majority
to the Capitol. Unfortunately, the people were unresponsive.
Most of the races being contested did not turn on the international issue Wilson had raised, but on far more provincial
issues raised by far more provincial actors. On the basis of
these local issues and the strength of their local candidates,
Republicans swept into control of the Senate, turning a forty-
two to fifty-three deficit in the Sixty-fifth Congress into a
forty-eight to forty-seven advantage in the Sixty-sixth. In the
House, the GOP widened a precarious six-vote advantage
into one of forty-six votes (237–191). More importantly, since
Wilson had tried to make the election a plebiscite on his peace
proposals, the Republican leadership interpreted the returns
as a resounding mandate to oppose the Treaty of Versailles
and, especially, the League of Nations. In fact, there probably
was no *national* mandate.

With the American election barely over, President Wilson,
in an unprecedented move, left for Paris on December 4,
1918, to lead the nation's peace delegation in person. After
much negotiation and compromise among the world leaders
assembled in the mirrored halls of Versailles, a final peace
treaty was agreed upon and signed on June 28, 1919. It was
based, more or less, on Wilson's proposals and included a
planned League of Nations, a new, international organization
of the world's sovereign states designed to act as an international policeman and judge for the purpose of avoiding future wars, peacefully resolving future international conflicts,
and beginning a process of international disarmament. Although Wilson had the support of such internationally
minded Republicans as former President William Howard
Taft, the GOP's congressional leadership—including Senator
Henry Cabot Lodge, whose personal enmity for Wilson was
empowered by his new position as chairman of the Senate

Foreign Relations Committee—was firmly set in opposition to the Treaty of Versailles, feeling the public had repudiated the treaty's principles in the last election. Wilson and the treaty's supporters argued passionately that the success of a peaceful postwar world order depended upon American leadership in the League. "Dare we reject it and break the heart of the world?" Wilson asked the Senate on July 10.[9] Lodge and the other opponents of the treaty so dared. They viewed the treaty provisions as calling for unwise and illegal abdications of American sovereignty and foolishly committing the United States to interfere in the sovereignty of other nations.

The political battle over the treaty raged through the summer months of 1919. Despite the fact that ratification was supported by such diverse papers as the *Boston Globe*, the *Philadelphia Inquirer*, and the *Des Moines Register*, and that polls showed that 87 percent of newspaper editors around the country favored either outright or conditional ratification, Lodge and his "irreconcilable" allies in the Senate were unmoved, claiming true public opinion had manifested itself at the ballot box. In September, both President Wilson and treaty opponents began stumping around the country trying to rally public support for their position. This effort almost killed the president. Still weak from a case of influenza he had contracted in Paris and further worn down by the ambitious, national whistle-stop tour he undertook, Wilson suffered a series of strokes from September 25 through October 1. Partially paralyzed, he lay confined for two months in the White House as the Senate debated and, on November 19, 1919, finally voted down his cherished treaty.

In the final analysis, I think it fair to say that Wilson's vision for the future—a vision that had informed America's entry into the war, might have spared the world the horrors of a

---

[9]Quoted in Alexander L. and Juliette L. George, *Woodrow Wilson and Colonel House* (New York: John Day, 1956), 273.

second "war to end all wars," and certainly would have provided for a more stable international order—was casually dashed by the American electorate in the midterm elections of 1918. Although they had backed Wilson staunchly during the course of the war and—we have reason to believe— broadly supported his call for a League of Nations, the American people, for parochial reasons unrelated to the League, derailed the president's treaty efforts. As a result, the business of World War I was left largely unfinished, and the Republicans were allowed to withdraw the nation into a dangerous isolationism.

The second example of the deleterious impacts of midterm elections can be found in Franklin Roosevelt's experience in 1938. Roosevelt had swept into the White House in 1932 with a landslide election victory that had extremely long coattails. Democrats picked up a "whopping" ninety-nine seats in the House and twelve in the Senate, giving the new president a large working majority in each chamber. Furthermore, the Democratic margins had been expanded in both the midterm election of 1934 (when the party added nine seats in the House and ten in the Senate) and the presidential election year of 1936 (during which Democrats added six more Senate and eleven House seats). As a result of this string of election victories, in the Seventy-fifth Congress (1937–1938), Roosevelt's party enjoyed a 331–89 edge in the House and a 76–16 advantage in the Senate. These figures are deceptive, however, as FDR was soon to learn. Despite an overwhelming partisan majority on paper, many of the Democrats in the Congress were conservatives who often voted with the Republicans against extension of the president's New Deal programs. After a promising start in January 1937, and in the wake of his failed "Court-packing plan," Roosevelt's legislative agenda quickly bogged down in the Seventy-fifth Congress. Even though the president personally and his policies generally enjoyed great public popularity, the conservative coalition in the Congress allowed only a small agricultural program, a weak wage-hour bill and a poorly funded housing bill through the legislative wringer. The New Deal, as a program for the general welfare, seemed to be grinding to a halt, despite the huge Democratic majorities in the Capitol.

Assaying the situation early in 1938, Roosevelt came to two conclusions. First, he decided that Americans really did need, want, and deserve a broadening of the liberal, New Deal legislation he was proposing. Eight to ten million citizens remained unemployed, and much of the economic suffering brought on by the Depression remained unrelieved. Second, and more important for our discussion, he determined that some kind of radical action was needed if his proposals were ever to clear the Congress. By the spring of the year the president had settled on his course of action: he would break with previous executive etiquette and his own pledge of noninterference in local elections to campaign in the midterm against Democrats who were not adequately supportive of the New Deal. In essence, he had decided to purge the party of its conservative congressional elements.

Roosevelt began his assault on the conservatives in a fireside chat broadcast to the nation late in June. "As the head of the Democratic Party," he said, "charged with the responsibility of the definitely liberal declaration of principles set forth in the 1936 Democratic platform, I feel that I have every right to speak in those few instances where there may be a clear issue between candidates for a Democratic nomination involving those principles, or involving a clear misuse of my name."[10] "[T]hose few instances" took the president on a whistle-stop tour around the nation, stumping for liberal Democratic congressional candidates.

While Roosevelt did his best to make the election a vote of confidence in the New Deal, numerous local issues dominated individual races. Around the nation brush fires of paro-

---

[10]See James MacGregor Burns, *Roosevelt: The Lion and the Fox* (New York: Harcourt, Brace and Co., 1956), 360.

chial electoral concerns broke out, and the president was unable to contain them. In South Carolina, the issue turned on a racist theme, with "Cotton Ed" Smith raising the banner of white supremacy and his opponent Johnson countering that Smith had once voted "to let a big buck nigger sit next to your wife or daughter on a train."[11] In Michigan and other midwestern states, strikes and labor unrest became the central issue; in Pennsylvania and Massachusetts, it was political corruption. Many races in California became embroiled in the local politics of a state pension plan; in Rhode Island and Connecticut, the key issues were a racetrack scandal and a highway squabble, respectively. New Jersey's congressional races turned on the tyrannical reputation of the state's political boss, Frank Hague. In short, the midterm elections Roosevelt wanted to make a popular referendum on the New Deal turned into largely provincial races dominated, as usual, by local issues. The results were nearly disastrous for the New Deal. Not only did the Republicans almost double their strength in the House (picking up eighty seats) and gain six new senators, but most of the anti-New Deal Democrats whom Roosevelt had campaigned against had been able to control the campaign agenda and had easily won reelection. After the electoral smoke had cleared, the liberal, pro-New Deal faction in the House had been cut in half.

The policy consequences were predictable. While the conservative coalition on the Hill could not muster the two-thirds majority necessary to override Roosevelt's veto and abolish the New Deal, it had more than enough votes to prevent any extension of liberal programs. Relief appropriations, bills to fund self-liquidation projects, and proposals to lend money to housing programs foundered on the shoals of conservative opposition in the House. The conservative congressional leadership flexed its political muscle, instigating investigations of liberal agencies, blocking the appointment of key ad-

[11] Ibid., 364.

ministrative personnel, and limiting the annual appropriations for the general funds of many critical New Deal offices.
The result of this political deadlock was an economic stalemate. After its promising spasm of success, the New Deal
faced, in the Seventy-sixth Congress, a conservative phalanx
aligned against it. Much of the new, inspired program Roosevelt envisioned to confront the nation's new, horrific economic problems could not pass conservative litmus tests and,
hence, congressional muster. The New Deal, I contend, was
only half dealt and would remain unfinished largely because
the conservative coalition could, with prima facie plausibility,
claim it had been rejected by the public in the midterm elections of 1938.

There are numerous other examples, such as the faltering
of the Great Society effort after 1966 or the sputtering of President Reagan's planned conservative revolution following the
elections of 1982, that we could add to the list. Like so many
other mechanisms built into our constitutional order, midterm elections fragment power and make steady, rational,
planned leadership quite difficult. As a result, our quality of
governance and our ability, as a society, to address the many
problems we face have been undermined in the past and will
continue to be frustrated in the future. Our institutionally
factionalized system, stripped of its integrative partisan cata-
lyst, has proven inefficient at both representing the majority
will and protecting the rights of minorities. The upshot is that
our governmental system—for all its accomplishments—has
not, in this modern era, proven worthy of the faith placed in it
by the American people. It has contributed to an enormous
waste of human talent and to the squandering of countless
opportunities to improve society; it has thwarted majority
will, stymied popular leaders, derailed badly needed policies,
ill protected minority rights, and rendered us largely unable
to plan for crises before they break and incapable of any but
incomplete responses after they are upon us. Intellectually,
the triumph of the Constitution of 1787 over the party ma-

jority/party minority system outlined above has left us with political institutions that are incompetent at transforming our values into viable, efficient, progressive policies. Where others, more optimistic than I, perhaps, see a glass that is half full and congratulate themselves on our progress, I see a glass that is not only half empty, but leaking. Not one to despair, however, I have some suggestions for how the glass might be repaired and refilled.

I support two basic reforms for our political system. First, we must strengthen our political parties; and, second, we must amend our Constitution to allow for effective partisan rule. I am not so naïve as to think that all of the proposals I will outline are politically practical or that they can easily be implemented. I am well aware of the difficulties that inhere in the reforms I champion, and I am conscious of the many powerful interests arrayed against them. I do, however, believe there are important intellectual benefits to discussing how our system may be improved and ruminating on the merits of various alternatives. I consider myself a political realist in the positive sense of that term, in that I try neither to overestimate nor underestimate human potential. The legacy of the founders convinces me that we are capable, if we but resolve ourselves to do so, of critical political analysis and creative political planning. Before any reform, any "creative political plan," can be implemented, it must first be envisioned, and that is what I suggest we do now—envisage what beneficial reforms would look like.

First, under the general rubric of party reform, I would suggest four changes. Initially, we need to decrease our reliance on direct primaries and reinvigorate the party convention— on the local, state, and national levels—as the principal organ for the selection of political nominees. Although primaries bring more people into the candidate-selection process, they have not democratized the procedure as much as once thought and have estranged the party leadership from the candidates eventually selected. In the highly touted New Hampshire and

California Democratic presidential primaries—the ones that attract the *most* interest—only some 14 percent of eligible voters go to the polls. With that small a percentage actually voting, there is no guarantee that the candidates chosen will have true popular appeal.

In a convention-based system, while fewer people may actually take part in the process, those who do will have a richer experience and, since they are the most committed and loyal elements within the party, they will take greater pains to select competent and competitive candidates. In addition, the primary system limits the influence of the party's elected officials in the selection of nominees, and, therefore, their sense of common purpose. As the Democratic Party's Commission on Presidential Nomination (the so-called Hunt Commission, named after its chair, former North Carolina Governor Jim Hunt) concluded in 1982: "Primaries have proliferated, removing decision-making power from party caucuses and conventions. Our national convention has been in danger of what one critic has called a 'rubber stamp electoral college.' To an alarming extent our party's public officials have not participated in and thus have felt only a limited responsibility for our recent national conventions."[12] In a more vibrant convention system, elected political elites would have a greater say in the nomination process, encouraging them to become more active in the party and contributing to a stronger partisan linkage among the party's elected officials. The result could be an enhanced willingness and capability to form effective governing coalitions with other partisan officeholders.

With a stronger system of state and local caucuses and conventions, the number of presidential primaries could be greatly reduced, saving a good deal of money, among other advantages. I would recommend perhaps ten state primaries,

[12] For a discussion of the Hunt Commission's recommendations, see David E. Price, *Bringing Back the Parties* (Washington, D.C.: Congressional Quarterly Press, 1984), 159–79.

spread in a representative fashion around the country—several in the large western states, several in the South, a few in the Midwest, and some in the Northeast. Unfortunately, though there is some sympathy for limiting the number of primaries, if the move to Super Tuesday is any indication, I fear the current trend may be toward a single, national primary. This, to my mind, would be disastrous; it would compound the problems of the numerous state primaries and totally strip the party leadership of any hand in choosing presidential nominees. A national primary could be the final death knell for competitive American political parties.

To extend the football analogy I drew earlier, my proposal for more conventions and fewer primaries would take the player selection and play calling responsibilities away from the fans and return them to the coaching staff. The result, in my estimation, would be a more competitive and representative party system. As Jeane Kirkpatrick has noted, "'open' participatory politics may turn out (as in 1972) to be less representative of party rank and file (and other voters) than conventions peopled by labor leaders, political 'bosses,' and public officials."[13] Given the recent presidential record of the Democratic Party, the most "participatory" of the two, and the wholesale partisan abandonment of the presidential tickets in 1968, 1972, 1980, and 1984, the suggestions I am making would seem to have considerable relevance to "practical politics."

The second partisan reform I favor would be a radical overhaul of our campaign-financing arrangements. Especially at the congressional level, the cost of running for public office has skyrocketed in recent years. While there are many reasons for this (more advanced and costly campaign techniques, the proliferation of primaries, spiraling media costs, population growth, the expansion in the number of potential

---

[13]Jeane Kirkpatrick, *The New Presidential Elite: Men and Women in National Politics* (New York: The Russell Sage Foundation, 1976), 330.

voters), the results are clear: the necessity for constant fund raising that ties candidates to well-heeled special interests and distracts officeholders from other, more important tasks. The amount of money spent in elections is truly staggering. In 1974 the average candidate for a House seat raised only $61,000. By 1982 that figure had risen to $222,000, with successful candidates spending nearly $450,000, on average, by 1984. Figures are even higher in the Senate, where average expenditures rose from $455,000, in 1972, to over $1,770,000, in 1982. Today, in competitive states, Senate races regularly cost in excess of $5 million. In the legendary 1984 race between Senator Jesse Helms and Governor Jim Hunt, in North Carolina, the candidates spent a total of $21 million.[14]

As costs have risen, so has the percentage of campaign support provided to candidates by special interests. In 1972 political action committees (PACs) provided only 14 percent of the average House candidate's finances and 12 percent of the average Senate candidate's financial backing. By 1984 those figures had risen to 37 and 19 percent, respectively, far outstripping levels of partisan support, which had tumbled over the twelve-year period. Many people worry that such heavy reliance on the financial support of special interests skews— or at least taints by giving the impression of skewing—the legislative process.

Witnessing the handwriting on the wall, Congress, in 1974, undertook efforts to reform election financing. Unfortunately, it badly botched the job. In the Federal Election Campaign Act (FECA) of 1974, it instituted a voluntary public-financing (tax-form checkoff) scheme for presidential races, which has been utilized by virtually every serious presidential contender since. Congress did not, however, vote to initiate a public-financing program for congressional elections, opting instead

[14]See Gary C. Jacobson, "Money in the 1980 and 1982 Congressional Elections," in *Money and Politics in the United States*, ed. Michael J. Malbin (Chatham, N.J.: Chatham House Publishers, 1984), 39.

for a set of spending limits for House and Senate races. The Supreme Court, reviewing the law in the 1976 case of *Buckley v. Valeo*, did not look favorably on the spending caps. Ruling that while Congress could place limits on campaign donations, the Court's majority held that the legislature—at least in the absence of public financing—could not limit a candidate's spending, since such spending was a form of political speech protected by the first amendment. To clarify the status of electoral laws in the wake of the Buckley decision, Congress in 1976 passed an amended FECA that set rather severe limits on campaign contributions (especially those coming from parties), but placed no cap on overall candidate spending. The predictable result has been the mushrooming expenditures and PAC growth already described.

Certainly one way to trim the badly overgrown hedge of congressional campaign spending would be to do what the Congress was loathe to do in 1974 and 1976—fund campaigns publicly. A public-financing scheme would seem to satisfy the Court's objection to spending caps and could be operated much like that used for presidential elections. There are, of course, those in Congress who object to such proposed reforms. Some incumbents tend to see public financing as giving a leg up to the challengers they would like to discourage from coming after their seats. More generally, congressmen are congressmen because they have been electorally successful under the rules of the present game and are, understandably, reluctant to see them changed.

I believe, however, we are beginning to see in the Congress a groundswell of support from members who have grown weary of spending so much of their time raising money for the next campaign. The financial imperative is so onerous that House members are engaged in a virtually constant fundraising campaign, and senators are having to devote an ever-increasing portion of their time to keeping their war chests full. Recent polls of and interviews with various congressmen and senators have shown that many would like to spend

more time on issues and less on fund raising, and some leading observers believe the recent rise in early congressional re-
tirements can be attributed to members who have grown
weary of their constant fund-raising responsibilities. Further
evidence of this groundswell can be seen in the fact that there
are currently a dozen or more campaign finance reform
bills—introduced by members as diverse as Tony Coelho,
Robert Byrd, Mo Udall, David Boren, and Mike Synar—being
considered by the Congress.

To my mind, what is critical in any kind of campaign finance reform is that it strengthen the position of our political
parties. This could be accomplished concomitantly with or independent of public matching funds, but if we are to rejuve-
nate our parties, making them more active, responsible, and
capable of maintaining coherent policy coalitions, we must
give them greater control over their candidates' campaign finances. We must, if we expect greater partisan loyalty and co-
alescence, render elected officials more reliant on their parties
for the sine qua non of elections, money.

This could be accomplished in a number of ways. First, the
limits on what parties may contribute to candidates could be
raised or scrapped altogether. Under current law, state and
national party committees may directly contribute a maxi-
mum of only $20,000 to each House candidate and $27,000
to each Senate candidate. As Roger Davidson and Walter
Oleszek have noticed, "[e]ven with contributions from several such [partisan] committees, these sums do not begin to
cover the cost of today's campaigns. Direct party contributions in 1982 amounted to only 6 percent in the average
House race and 1 percent in Senate races."[15] Even when partisan coordinated expenditures (for such campaign services
as polling, get-out-the-vote efforts, and advertisement production) are included—and they are limited to two cents for

---

[15] Roger H. Davidson and Walter J. Oleszek, *Congress and Its Members*. 2d
ed. (Washington, D.C.: Congressional Quarterly Press, 1985), 70.

each voting-aged person in Senate races, $18,440 in House contests—the parties' shares of overall campaign contributions remain small. They could and should be raised to allow a greater partisan role in campaign financing.

Second, in order to ensure that parties—rather than PACs or individuals—are the candidates' principal financiers, FECA and our tax codes could be revised to provide contributors with incentives to donate money to the parties rather than directly to individual candidates. This would not only make parties the financial clearinghouses for campaigns, but give them the wherewithal to reward partisan loyalty, enforce the party platform, and build party responsibility and accountability.

The third partisan reform I recommend concerns the manner in which we structure our ballots. One of the untoward consequences of our switch to the Australian ballot during the progressive era was, as I have already discussed, an increase in the instances of split-ticket voting. Politically, the consequences of split tickets are splits in the partisan control of the institutions of government. We no longer think it unusual, for instance, when we have Republican presidents in the White House and large Democratic majorities in one or both chambers of the Congress. What such splits do, however, is confuse the public and make accountability very difficult. A Republican president can, plausibly perhaps, blame the Democratic Congress for the government's deficits, scandals, military disasters, malaise, and so forth, while the Democrats in Congress are busy blaming the president for exactly the same ills. The public, caught in the middle, usually cannot decide who deserves the blame and whom to hold responsible. This situation could be alleviated by facilitating straight-party voting. States and locales that use office-bloc ballots could be persuaded to adopt party-bloc ballots, and innovative steps could be taken to encourage straight-party voting, while making ticket splitting more difficult.

Fourth and finally on my list of suggested partisan reforms, something must be done to strengthen the position of the party minority, the party out of power. At the core of the problem is that presidential systems like ours lack one of the principal advantages of the parliamentary system, the shadow cabinet. In our system, the opposition party has no single spokesperson, no one to articulate its platform and explain why its agenda is better for the nation than the president's. Instead, there are numerous presidential hopefuls, each claiming to speak for the party, running around the country, shouting at one another and the public in a cacophony of voices about different issues. The public is, justifiably, often confused by all this and uncertain as to what alternatives it really faces. Informed political choices can hardly be made under such adverse conditions. While I have few concrete recommendations regarding how to address and mitigate this problem, it is one that deserves our attention and imagination.

That, then, is my agenda for strengthening our political parties. By themselves, however, these partisan reforms will not be enough to ensure a return to a party majority/party minority system. While I have no particular fondness for tampering with the Constitution and generally discourage those who would attempt to solve all our problems by the amendment process, I do believe it is necessary to alter the Constitution moderately in order to strengthen the party system fundamentally. Certain institutional arrangements have to be modified—slightly, I would stress—if we are to see a rebirth of strong, responsible, accountable political parties.

First, although I do not, for the reasons I have outlined previously, advocate a switch to a parliamentary system, I believe we would be well served by allowing joint executive-legislative appointments. Joint appointments, of course, have a faint parliamentary flavor to them and would require amending article one, section six, of the Constitution, which states that "no Person holding any Office under the United States, shall be a Member of either House [of Congress] during his

Continuance in Office." The advantages offered by such joint appointments, however, are numerous. To begin with, they would tend to stabilize both personnel and policies. Instead of having to recruit members outside government to fill key cabinet posts, a new president could call upon his party's elected policy experts in the Congress to provide his administration with their expertise and authority. It is certainly plausible to think that joint legislative-executive appointments would bring better, more experienced, more knowledgeable people into the service of the executive branch.

More importantly, perhaps, joint appointments would also provide a valuable linkage between the president and the Congress. A senator or congressman sitting on the cabinet would be in a position to act as a medium between the administration and the president's party in the Congress. Institutionally, he would be in a strong position to relay congressional and partisan sentiment to the president and take back to the Congress the president's concerns and rationale. Joint appointments would concentrate power in the hands of a few individuals, but could provide a key linkage mechanism between the otherwise estranged executive and legislative branches.

Second, I favor a four-year term for members of the Congress, concurrent with the presidential term. As I have noted, the principal problem with "off-year" biennial congressional elections is that they tend to be decided on very parochial grounds. Among the numerous advantages promised by the four-year term (for example, lower election costs, less preoccupation with fund raising), several deserve mention here. First, a president would have four years to work with the Congress he came into office with and would not face the prospect of having his agenda derailed by the results of a local election two years into his tenure. Second, members of Congress would be more firmly linked to their parties' presidential candidates. They would know that in every election year, their electoral success would depend largely upon who was at the top of the ticket and how successful that person had been or promised to be in the White House. The four-year term, in short, would give the parties' congressional elements a greater stake in their presidential candidates, forming firmer linkages between the two. It would be a move toward collective authority and responsibility.

I should note, however, that regardless of the advantages of the four-year term, it faces stiff opposition on a number of fronts. Not only do many people of good will agree with the founders that the members of the House of Representatives must be "kept close to the people" and subject to their review every other year, many senators have less pure motives for opposing any such amendment. As it stands, with members of the House facing reelection every second year, they must forfeit their congressional seats to run for the Senate. If they held a four-year term, on the other hand, they would find themselves free in the middle of their term to challenge for a Senate seat. A majority of Senators, I suspect, or at least a large enough number to block a constitutional amendment, would just as soon not hand their colleagues in the House the option of a free run at their seats.

Another constitutional reform we should consider is an expansion of the impeachment power. Currently, under the provisions of article two, section four of the Constitution, a president may be removed from office by impeachment only after conviction on charges of "Treason, Bribery, or other high Crimes and Misdemeanors." That is a fairly short list, and the founders wanted it that way. They wanted to insulate, as much as possible, the executive from the legislative branch. With the breakdown of parties in the modern era, however, this insulation has further contributed to our malady of government by deadlock. Too often, in the recent past, we have seen situations in which the sitting president, while having committed no serious crime, has lost the confidence of the people, the backing of Congress, and the power to govern. In our system, regardless of the vacuum of power this leaves, there is no constitutional mechanism by which to remove the incumbent. We have no functional equivalent of the vote of no confidence, and we need one. Given the kinds of tremendous crises that may await us in the near future, this need is great and growing.

A constitutional amendment authorizing a presidential vote of no confidence should at least give the Congress, acting on the authority of an extraordinary majority, the power to impeach and remove a sitting president who has lost the ability to guide and govern the nation. Not only would such an amendment allow the removal of a politically disabled president, it could enhance interbranch and intraparty cooperation by giving the executive added incentives to cooperate with, instead of fighting against, the legislature.

Finally, I believe we should repeal the twenty-second amendment, which limits a president to two terms of office. This ill-conceived amendment was the product of the Eightieth Congress, elected in 1946 and the first since 1931 to have a Republican majority. Having, in its eyes, suffered grievous setbacks at the hands of Franklin Roosevelt during his unprecedented four terms as president, the GOP majority quickly set about ensuring no president would ever have such long-lasting power again, passing the twenty-second amendment on March 24, 1947.

The amendment is ill-conceived, I contend, because it guarantees that second-term presidents will be politically impotent lame ducks. When it is certain that a president will not stand for reelection, he automatically loses much of the political capital he needs to govern. He has little to trade, and congressmen and bureaucrats have little to fear from him. He becomes what we used to call in the military a short-timer, someone who can safely be ignored. Rescission of the twenty-second amendment would give a second-term president considerably more latitude and political leverage. The possibility that he could run for a third term or even at some later date come out of retirement to run for a nonconsecutive term would, in effect, enhance his political standing as a powerful partisan figure for the entirety of his tenure in office. Repeal would be another move toward more responsible government.

As I have emphasized throughout, the founders are worthy of our approbation because they are worthy of our emulation. We should honor them not so much for what they accomplished, which was no mean feat, but for how they accomplished it. At a time when all the pressures and problems of a new nation weighed heavily upon them, they found within themselves the intelligence and the imagination to create a new political order. They were capable of distancing themselves from the then and there, of looking beyond their own immediate interests, and of mentally tracing through the implications of government to create a Constitution that manifested their values in their institutions. In the here and now, however, we must not allow the grandeur of their accomplishment to obscure the facts that, over the course of two hundred years, our values have broadened and strengthened more quickly than the institutions they bequeathed us, so that the two are currently badly out of step. We have, in effect, an eighteenth-century set of governmental institutions that cannot adequately process our society's twentieth-century values and expectations. If we are to ensure, "for ourselves and our posterity," the blessings of majority rule tempered by the protection of minority rights, we must begin to replicate the founders' method and to discuss ways our governmental institutions may be recalibrated to take better account of these values. I have concluded that this can best be accomplished through a rejuvenation of our political parties and a revitalization of party majority/party minority governance.

I hope my arguments have encouraged you to consider seriously the relative merits of my proposals and perhaps develop some others that have not occurred to me. Only through an intense effort at institutional analysis and intellectual leadership can we begin the vital constitutional dialogue our situation demands and prove ourselves worthy of the legacy left us by the framers.

INDEX